Perfect
JOB SEARCH
STRATEGIES

Over **100** proven strategies
for getting the job you want in
today's challenging market

TOM JACKSON

Perfect
JOB SEARCH
STRATEGIES

Over **100** proven strategies
for getting the job you want in
today's challenging market

TOM JACKSON

PIATKUS

Dedication

This book is dedicated to Dick Bolles, the passionate humanist, the spiritual pragmatist, the outstanding spokesperson of the right to a fulfilling livelihood, and the nonstop author of the most important book of its kind: *What Color Is Your Parachute?* Thanks, Dick.

First published in the UK in 1994 by
Judy Piatkus (Publishers) Ltd,
5 Windmill Street, London W1P 1HF

Reprinted 1995

A catalogue record for this book is available from the British Library

ISBN 0–7499–1312–6

Printed & bound in Great Britain by
The Bath Press, Bath, Avon

Acknowledgments

Bill Buckingham has been a true partner with me in the construction of this book. His input has gone to the essence of the material, the design of the forms, and the layout. He has worked unceasingly, as is his style in everything he undertakes, to contribute to the quality of the final product, Megan Denver is due a big thank you for her work on the Mac, and Jerry Lee and Ruth French for minding the shop while I toiled.

Thanks also to John Lockwood for assisting with anglicisation of parts of this book for my UK readers.

Chris and Andy should be awarded the "sons of the year" citation for containing (moderately) their impatience with a dad who was on a mission.

Contents

Introduction

Welcome to *Perfect Job Search Strategies*—a book designed to give you answers to more than one hundred situations, challenges, and turning points in your search for the job you want. Unlike most job search books, this volume is not designed to be *read*—as in starting at page 1 and moving through one chapter at a time until the last few pages have led you to your job search destination—the employment offer. This is a book of answers and strategies designed to meet the job needs at hand.

Key to the use of this book are the two indexes at the front: the *Index to Situations*, in which you identify a job search situation or problem and are then referred to sections dealing with strategies and actions to cope with that situation; and the *Index to Exercises*, in which you identify particular payoffs or outcomes you want and are referred to a pen-and-paper exercise or form designed to help you meet that need.

This is a book of strategic action. Simply knowing what should be done, or how something works, is not enough to get you the job you want in a difficult market. The book is designed to guide you to intelligent action each step of the way.

The actions, exercises, and principles presented in these pages come from more than a dozen years of practice with job seekers at all levels and in many fields. This does not mean that you need to follow them slavishly. They are yours to modify, adapt, ignore, or follow in detail as they are. We do suggest that you fall in with the intent of the strategy or exercise and spend enough time with each to determine the rationale and principles involved. Be willing to stretch yourself with each step in the process, despite the obstacles and resistance which will naturally arise.

And let *Perfect Job Search Strategies* lead you to a perfect job.

Tom Jackson

Index to Exercises

It is only by undertaking a series of strategic actions that you will systematically keep your perfect job search on target. The following Index to Exercises—including pen-and-paper planning forms and checklists—is organized by the value to you, the name and number of the exercise, and the page number. Use these exercises in any order based on your own needs. Feel free to modify, adjust, expand, or take them as they are. As you will see, each exercise requires attention and energy on your part. The more you put into it, the bigger the return.

1. Knowing What You Want to Do

Value to You	Strategic Action Exercise	Page
Expanding personal satisfaction in your work	✍ 1: Career Success	3
Aligning your career goals with your values, ambitions, and interests	✍ 2: Job Satisfiers	5
Discovering the skills that make you unique	✍ 3: The Skills Detector	8
Discovering personal motivations that can enhance the satisfaction of your future work	✍ 4: The Pleasure Detector	8

2. Getting on the Fast Track: Jumping Hurdles to Success

3. Discovering the Hidden Job Market

4. Power CVs

5. Power Cover Letters

6. Getting Inside for Interviews

7. Turning Interviews into Offers

8. Strategic Follow-up

9. Closing the Deal and Negotiation Compensation

Index to Situations

The following Index to Situations will guide you quickly to particular problems or questions that arise during your job search. The primary reference for each situation appears first; other references follow.

To make this index even easier to use, simply cut along the vertical dotted lines on each of the following pages.

Job Search Situation	Strategies	
	Primary	Other
• I don't know what it takes to get hired in this economy.	1.6	4.4 5.3 7.5 7.6
• I feel depleted. My interest in work seems to have dried up.	1.11	
• I used to feel secure in my work. Not anymore!	1.8	3.4 1.12
• I'd love to give up the commuting and work at home.	1.9	3.3
• I want a job with more personal satisfaction and growth.	1.10	1.9
• I'm desperate for a job. What does it take to crack this tough market?	1.6	7.12 7.6
• I've always seen myself in terms of my qualifications and profession. Now my field is hurting. How do I get out of this trap?	1.12	1.1 1.2 1.3 1.13
• I'm not sure of the kind of job I want.	1.2	1.4 1.9 3.3
• I'm not good at "selling" myself.	1.6	1.2 4.2 7.5
• My degree doesn't have the clout it used to.	1.7	1.3 1.8
• I've had many jobs that didn't work out for me.	1.2	1.3
• Is it better to be open for any job prospect or to focus on a specific target?	1.4	1.6 2.1 3.3
• I'm tempted to go underground until the economy improves.	1.13	1.12 2.1
• A dream job is just fantasy, and this is reality. I don't want to kid myself.	1.1	1.2 1.12 1.13
• There are no real jobs near where I live.	1.5	1.6 2.9 3.1
• There are so many different directions to consider, I'm not sure what I want.	1.4	1.1 1.2 1.3
• There are a lot of people out there with the same skills and qualifications that I have. How do I find a competitive edge?	1.3	1.6 1.8

| | Strategies | |
Job Search Situation	Primary	Other
• Finding a job is a lonely experience. I can't do it all by myself.	**2.5**	3.4
• How can I expect an employer to be interested in me when my whole industry is downsizing?	**2.8**	1.6 3.2
• How do I keep my spirits from flagging during my long job search?	**2.10**	2.5 2.7
• I don't have the time to do a perfect job search.	**2.2**	2.5
• I've been out of work for months and feel powerless to influence the employer's decisions.	**2.4**	6.1
• I have a hard time dealing with rejection. I lose the enthusiasm to keep looking.	**2.7**	1.12 2.5
• I look in the help-wanted ads, but there's nothing there that interests me.	**2.9**	3.1
• I'm doing things to look for a job but never seem to get anywhere.	**2.2**	2.5 2.7
• I don't want anyone to know I'm out of work.	**2.5**	
• I've done well with my career, but I'm lousy at conducting my own job search.	**2.1**	1.6 4.2
• How can I manage a period of unemployment with no income?	**2.5**	
• I'm obviously qualified for the jobs I apply for. Why aren't they calling me back?	**2.1**	1.6 4.2
• I need to organize my time in the job search.	**2.2**	
• I've tried the traditional job search strategies but with no success.	**2.6**	2.7 6.2
• I resent that it's not the best person who's hired; it's the one who knows how to play the game.	**2.1**	1.6 4.2
• There's no one out there who needs me right now.	**2.4**	1.6 3.5 3.6
• These are bad times. Employers aren't hiring.	**2.8**	2.9 3.1 3.2
• They'll never take me seriously because I am (too young, too old, a woman, a minority . . .).	**2.3**	2.5 2.10

| | Strategies | |
Job Search Situation	Primary	Other
• There are no jobs in my community.	**3.5**	2.9 3.2
• I've tried all the firms I know of in my field. What else is there?	**3.3**	3.5 3.6
• Every time I answer an advertised opening, there seems to be a waiting list of candidates. How can I get a head start?	**3.1**	3.2 3.9
• How can my colleagues and associates best help in my job search?	**3.4**	2.5 3.6
• How do I find out about jobs in other places?	**3.3**	3.4 3.9
• How can I tell whether an employer prospect is worth the attention it will take to get inside?	**3.6**	3.7
• I can't find anything relevant in the employment classifieds.	**3.1**	2.9 3.2
• Isn't contacting employers directly too pushy? I'd rather use the mail.	**3.8**	3.6 6.2 6.3
• I have a good business idea for some company. How do I capitalize on it?	**3.2**	3.6 3.10 7.6
• I have an offer in which I'm moderately interested. Should I accept it or wait for something better to come along?	**3.7**	9.1
• I want a job in a major corporation where all the money and opportunity are.	**3.9**	
• It's easy to get information on large companies. What about the small ones?	**3.5**	3.3 3.6 3.9
• My previous jobs didn't work out too well. I don't want to repeat the same mistakes.	**3.7**	1.2
• Perhaps I should start my own business.	**3.10**	

| | Strategies | |
Job Search Situation	Primary	Other
• How do I include unpaid work experience on my CV?	4.3	4.5
• How much of my history do I need on my CV?	4.1	4.3 4.5
• I have a computer. Do CV writing software packages offer an advantage?	4.7	
• I just graduated from college. How do I get employers to take me seriously?	4.8	
• I was unemployed for a year and a half. How do I cover this gap on my CV?	4.8	
• I'm changing careers, and my past experience is not relevant to my new job target area.	4.5	4.6
• How should I emphasize my education?	4.8	4.3 4.5
• My work experience could take a book to describe fully.	4.3	4.6
• I've spent the last fifteen years as a mother and homemaker. What can I say on a CV?	4.8	4.3
• I'm in my fifties and my CV clearly reveals my age. Is this OK?	4.8	
• I'm just starting out and don't have a lot of work experience.	4.5	4.3 4.8
• I'm not a good writer. What style should I use on my CV?	4.6	
• My CV is too long and I can't find anything to cut out.	4.6	4.4
• My CV looks as if I can't hold down job.	4.5	
• My CV reads like a job description What can I do to strengthen it?	4.2	4.4
• Should I have one general-purpose CV or a different one for each job opening?	4.4	
• Should I include my true career goal even if it doesn't match the job I am applying for?	4.8	4.3 4.4
• I have a gap in my employment that sticks out.	4.5	
• Should I list references on my CV?	4.8	
• Should I list salary requirements on my CV?	4.6	
• What personal information should I include?	4.6	4.2 4.4

	Strategies	
Job Search Situation	Primary	Other
• I don't know whom to address in my cover letter. Will "Dear Sir or Madam" suffice?	**5.2**	
• How do I get names and addresses of key people to send my CV to?	**5.2**	
• Why is it necessary to include a cover letter with my CV?	**5.1**	
• My cover letter just repeats information included on my CV?	**5.3**	5.1
• What can I say in a cover letter to attract an employer's attention?	**5.1**	1.6 4.2 4.4
• What's the best way to have my cover letter lead to action?	**5.4**	

Job Search Situation	Strategies	
	Primary	Other
• How can I present myself so that the employer will call me for an interview?	**6.1**	1.6 7.6
• How do I get through the secretary to speak to the boss?	**6.3**	3.4 3.6
• I always get the same response from the personnel department: There are no job openings right now.	**6.3**	1.5 3.6 6.2
• I choke up when speaking to strangers on the phone.	**6.3**	3.8
• I've contacted as many employers as I can think of. What more can I do?	**6.4**	3.5 3.6 3.7
• I've narrowed down my prospects to fifteen potential employers. What now?	**6.2**	6.3 6.4
• I've sent out at least fifty CVs and have not heard from anyone.	**6.2**	
• It's hard to keep up my energy. I need a job more than employers need me.	**6.1**	2.2 2.4
• Few people return my phone calls.	**6.2**	2.6 8.4
• What is the best time to get through to the hiring managers?	**6.3**	

Job Search Situation	Strategies			
	Primary	Other		
• During interviews, I can't tell how well I am coming across.	7.4	7.9		
• How can I anticipate questions that might come up in the interview?	7.10	3.3	4.4	7.2
• How can I improve my ability to communicate?	7.9	4.2	7.2	7.5
• What do I wear to the interview?	7.8			
• I often leave the interview not knowing what will happen next.	7.13	8.1	8.5	
• I don't feel like an equal participant in an interview. The employer has all the control.	7.1	2.4	7.9	
• I feel as if I'm bragging when I speak about my accomplishments.	7.7	1.6	4.2	7.5
• I get the sense that the interviewer has made up his mind against me. How can I change this?	7.6	1.6	7.9	
• I go into interviews knowing very little about the job or the employer.	7.2	3.3	4.4	
• I just had the worst interview of my life. What can I do to rescue it?	7.15	8.1	8.5	
• I got the sense that the employer wasn't paying 100% attention to me in the interview.	7.9	7.5	7.12	
• I never know what questions to ask.	7.3	7.5	7.6	
• I know I've got what it takes, but I lack experience. What do I say in an interview?	7.11	1.3	1.6	
• I never know if I'm being too pushy.	7.7	2.4	6.1	
• I think of the best things to say after the interview. What can I do?	7.15	7.2	7.14	8.2
• I'm desperate for a job, and I'm afraid that it shows in an interview.	7.12	1.6		
• Interviews make me nervous.	7.1	2.3	2.10	
• Most of the time I wing my way through interviews.	7.1	7.2		
• Should I ask questions about salary and benefits at the first interview?	7.12			
• What can I do to prepare for a tough interview?	7.14	7.2	7.5	7.6
• What can I do to make a good first impression at an interview?	7.7	7.8		
• What can I say about myself in an interview to stimulate the employer's interest?	7.5	1.6	7.6	
• What's the best way to make a strong impression at the end of an interview?	7.13			

| | Strategies | |
Job Search Situation	Primary	Other
• After the interview I realized that some of my questions weren't answered.	**8.3**	
• I've followed up after an interview and still haven't heard from the company. When do I give up?	**8.4**	8.5
• The employer is hesitating about offering me the job. What can I do?	**8.4**	8.2
• The interview process has dragged on for weeks. What can I do to speed it up?	**8.4**	8.2
• What can I do to improve future interviews?	**8.1**	8.5
• What can I say in a follow-up letter that will increase my chances of being hired?	**8.2**	8.5

Job Search Situation	Strategies	
	Primary	Other
• How can I convince an employer that I'm worth more than the standard salary range?	**9.2**	1.6
• How can I evaluate a job offer to see if it is right for me?	**9.1**	1.9
• I feel embarrassed to ask for a higher salary.	**9.1**	9.2
• I feel trapped in low-paying jobs. What can I do to move ahead?	**9.7**	1.10
• I have children to take care of and don't want a traditional 9-to-5 job.	**9.6**	1.9
• I just got a job offer, but the salary is below my target.	**9.5**	3.7 9.3 9.4
• I really want a job but am told I have to take a salary cut. How should I handle this?	**9.5**	9.4
• I'm starting a new career. How do I know what the right salary is?	**9.3**	3.3 3.6
• Is it acceptable to negotiate work hours and work style before accepting a job?	**9.6**	1.9
• The employer asked me to name my salary. What if I come in too low or too high?	**9.3**	9.4
• The employer described a salary range. Should I ask for the middle?	**9.3**	9.4
• Times are tough. I don't want to push for a salary that will bump me out of the picture.	**9.2**	9.5 9.7
• We've gone around on salary negotiations and we haven't yet agreed. Should I give in?	**9.5**	

Knowing What You
Want to Do

Most job searches begin with the question, Who am I, and what am I going to do about it? This chapter answers that question, addresses issues of personal values and satisfaction, and describes the process of transforming work from drudgery to self-expression.

This chapter suggests that you take a responsible, qualitative look at your future to make your work life meet the demands of your personal agenda— not the other way around. Here we ask you to create career targets that are energizing and satisfying to you.

We operate from the principle that there is no scarcity of jobs. In an ever-changing, dynamic economy, there is no scarcity of problems and opportunities that individuals can change into job targets and job possibilities. We stress that personal development of capabilities and skills leads to productive career development. By learning how to shape your own job in the multiple dimensions of location, role, task, hours, compensation, and work style, you can discover that new work relationships are possible and ever-expanding.

The ideal job is one that keeps working for *you*, that supports your personal values and outward material needs and makes a contribution to the world in which you live. As you learn to value internal qualities— versatility, integrity, creativity, and interpersonal skills—as much as learned skills and degrees, you develop the ability to adapt to a multifaceted, changing career marketplace with your personal integrity intact.

The truly creative job search takes courage. It takes the willingness to challenge things that are familiar to you and to stretch beyond known limits. The truly creative job search has you, the beneficiary and the responsible party, in the driver's seat, doing both the navigating and the powering toward a personal career vision.

Job Search Principles

1.1 Work is not a job to fill; it is what you do with your life.

1.2 The job search starts with a look inside, an inventory of your most personal values, interests, pleasures, and challenges.

1.3 Personal qualities are as important as learned skills in making your way in the work world.

1.4 A good job target is a work direction that combines your personal interests with your skills.

1.5 A job is an opportunity to solve a problem, and since there is no shortage of problems, there is no shortage of job opportunities.

1.6 The Universal Hiring Rule: Any employer will hire any individual as long as the employer is convinced that the hiring will bring more value than it costs.

1.7 Capability development leads to career development. By constantly enhancing your skills and your ability to deliver results, you enhance your versatility and the scope of your career as well as your earning potential.

1.8 Versatility is a prerequisite for personal security in the work environment of the nineties.

1.9 In today's work world it is possible to shape the job you want in many more dimensions than simply those of title, hours, and compensation.

1.10 The ideal job is the job that keeps on working for you.

1.11 The job market is global, multicultural, and multifaceted.

1.12 A truly creative job search takes courage, the willingness to challenge that which is familiar, and the desire to enter a new world of possibility.

1.13 You are responsible for the quality of your work life.

1.1 How to Spend 10,000 Days of Your Life

SITUATION

You will work approximately 10,000 days in your life. Given where you are now, you can choose a job to which you drag yourself every morning or a job that is stimulating and satisfying. When you work with enthusiasm and strive to create value for others as well as yourself, you generate more opportunities for yourself and establish long-term relationships with others in your field. In choosing to integrate work and life, you can earn respect at work and devote your time to those things that you value. However, taking this approach requires a stronger commitment to a strategic job search.

Job Search Principle to Follow

Work is not a job to fill; it is what you do with your life.

The quality of your work life directly influences the quality of your whole life. It is a mistake to separate the 9-to-5 aspects of life from the fullest expression of all of your needs, interests, and values. By taking the time to create a larger picture of who you are, you can increase the quality of life as well as achieve a good standard of living.

Strategic Actions

☞ Be willing to commit substantial extra time and energy to pursue a job that meets your values *and* pays a good salary. Are you willing?

☞ Examine for yourself, with a spouse or friend, the tradeoffs between high-stress, high-paying jobs and a quality way of working that supports your deepest values.

☞ Make a list of the things in past jobs that you most disliked doing or that were numbing or detrimental to your personal lifestyle.

☞ List those aspects of past jobs that were most rewarding.

☞ Think of two or three people you know who are in jobs that appear to nurture their self-respect and personal expression. What can you discover about how these people have integrated their professional with their personal needs?

☞ Ask yourself this question: How close is my life to the way I want it to be? Think of what you may need to do to bring your life closer to your ideals.

☞ Take some time to create a vision of what a successful future career might look like (see Exercise 1).

✍ **Exercise 1: CAREER SUCCESS**

Put an *x* on your current location in your 10,000-day work life.

Day 1 (early 20s)	Day 5,000 (mid-40s)	Day 10,000 (early 60s)
|– – – –|– + – –|– + – –|– + – –|– + – –|– + – –|– + – –|– + – –|– + – –|– – + – –|		

Sit back and take an imaginative look at a time approximately five years from now. You are working in an ideal job, a job that was once only a dream. You look forward to each day, knowing that your work is challenging and satisfying. Create a mental picture (or a real drawing) of you in this dream job.

FIVE YEARS FROM NOW: YOUR DREAM JOB

Imagine: It is now _____
(Future date)

What kind of organization are you working for?_____
_____

What does your work space or environment look like?_____
_____
_____
_____

What activities are you engaged in?_____
_____
_____
_____
_____
_____

This job makes strong use of your best skills and abilities. What are they?
_____
_____
_____
_____

You enjoy this job because it is aligned with one of your strongest interests. What is this interest?_____
_____

Last year, you received the Employee of the Year award for a most significant accomplishment. What was this accomplishment?_____
_____
_____

You have spent a lot of time improving your capability. What areas are you most proud of having developed?_____
_____

What three words would you use to describe the best qualities of this job?

_____

_____

_____

✍ Exercise 2: JOB SATISFIERS

Make a close examination of those things that are most meaningful and satisfying to you in the world of work, the things that keep your job and career goals aligned with your personal values, ambitions, and interests. Put a check next to the items that are most important to you. Next to each item you checked, write a short statement that expresses exactly what you want to attain or what gives you satisfaction.

EXAMPLE

____✓__ Making a contribution _Raise awareness about the environment._

____ Salary and income   _____

                                _____
____ Independence
                                _____
____ Creativity
                                _____
____ Power
                                _____
____ Leadership
                                _____
____ Flexibility
                                _____
____ Challenge
                                _____
____ Autonomy
                                _____

_____ Making a contribution

_____ Security

_____ Social status

_____ Advancement

_____ Recognition

_____ Intellectual stimulation

_____ Physical exertion

_____ Variety in activities

_____ Consistency in activities

_____ Making decisions

_____ Helping others

_____ Being part of a team

_____ Working under pressure

_____ Social contact

_____ Adventure

_____ Gaining respect

$\boxed{1.2}$ Discover Who You Are

Situation

You took a job that did not work out for you. "I didn't like working behind a desk . . . The work was too boring . . . The supervisor was always on my case . . . I just couldn't figure out how to use that computer system." We all have had at least one such job: You find yourself watching the clock for quitting time, you dread Monday mornings, you feel depleted.

In retrospect, you realize there was something in that job that was not aligned with your fundamental interests, values, and skills. There was little that excited you, challenged you to think, or gave you a chance to produce results that were meaningful to you. You were not the best match for the job. How do you avoid making such a mistake again?

Job Search Principle to Follow

The job search starts with a look inside, an inventory of your personal values, interests, pleasures, and challenges.

Do not focus only on education, skills, and experience in formulating your next job target. Consider earlier successes, personal pleasures, and ideals, and identify what has provided you with a full sense of self-expression and aliveness.

Strategic Actions

☞ Get in touch with a career counselor or placement office and find out what self-assessment tests are available to give you insight about how your skills and qualities correspond with different careers.

☞ Ask friends and colleagues to tell you what they consider to be your strongest and weakest qualities and capabilities.

☞ Find a copy of *The Career Discovery Project* by Gerald Sturman. (Aurum). Do the personal assessment exercises.

☞ Set aside thirty minutes and complete the following exercises designed to give you an inventory of some of your strongest skills and interests.

✍ Exercise 3: THE SKILLS DETECTOR

Basic skills are the foundation of your ability to get things done. We each have our own unique set of basic skills. Check any skill in which you consider yourself to be above average.

____ Reading	____ Organizing	____ Listening
____ Working with numbers	____ Cooking	____ Learning
____ Operating equipment	____ Decorating	____ Planning
____ Following instructions	____ Counseling	____ Teaching
____ Helping others	____ Using tools	____ Investigating
____ Supervising others	____ Making decisions	____ Writing
____ Working with animals	____ Communicating	____ Selling
____ Imagining/creating	____ Painting/drawing	____ Acting
____ Doing mechanical tasks	____ Working outdoors	____ Researching
____ Classifying	____ Meeting deadlines	____ Attending to
____ Singing	____ Repairing	detail
____ Performing	____ Negotiating	____ Conceptualizing
	____ Building	

_____ _____ _____

_____ _____ _____

_____ _____ _____

From this list select your top five basic skills:

1. _____
2. _____
3. _____
4. _____
5. _____

✍ Exercise 4: THE PLEASURE DETECTOR

In the spaces provided, check those activities that give you real pleasure, or probably would if you tried them.

____ To operate my own business	____ To work with machinery
____ To make a good bargain	____ To advise and consult
____ To do research	____ To work alone
____ To attend meetings	____ To sing or act
____ To persuade others	____ To design physical structures
____ To do routine tasks	____ To take care of people
____ To teach	____ To travel
____ To read	____ To entertain
____ To work for my community	____ To sell
____ To repair things	____ To work on a team

_____ To play sports
_____ To write
_____ To promote and publicize
_____ To do physical labor
_____ To work with numbers
_____ To serve people
_____ To solve people's problems
_____ To work in an office
_____ To dress casually
_____ To have regular hours
_____ To work irregular hours
_____ To work with my hands
_____ To invent and design
_____ To make decisions

_____ To work in politics
_____ To garden
_____ To lead groups
_____ To negotiate
_____ To work with money
_____ To supervise
_____ To learn new things
_____ To work outdoors
_____ To organize events
_____ To work for a small firm
_____ To work with a large company
_____ To operate technology
_____ To communicate by phone
_____ To work at night

Add more here:

_____   _____

_____   _____

_____   _____

From this list select your top five interests:
1. _____
2. _____
3. _____
4. _____
5. _____

✍ Exercise 5: PEAK EXPERIENCES

Part 1:
   Identify three peak experiences in your life, either professional or personal. Sit back and relax. Recall times of strong positive emotion, success, or great flashes of insight and clarity.

Examples: • Getting a coveted award or degree
   • Making a powerful presentation
   • Solving a very difficult problem
   • Mastering a new skill (computer, high jump, legal argument)

List your peak experiences in the following spaces.

Peak Experience 1:_____

   Associated skills:_____

   _____

   _____

Associated interests:_____   _____

_____

_____

Peak Experience 2:_____

    Associated skills:_____

_____

_____

    Associated interests:_____

_____

_____

Peak Experience 3:_____

    Associated skills:_____

_____

_____

    Associated interests:_____

_____

_____

Part 2:

Review each peak experience and think about what made that experience important to you. In the space provided for skills, list those skills that you enjoyed using or that challenged you to be successful. In the space provided for interests, describe how the peak experience related to your interests.

Part 3:

Return to Exercises 1 and 2. Review your top five skills and top five interests lists. Revise or change these lists to conform to what you have just discovered.

1.3 THE REAL POWER BEHIND YOUR WORK

SITUATION

From time to time you may feel trapped by limitations of education and experience. It may seem to you that you really don't know how to do anything beyond the skills required for your job. This is a common trap, a result of an overemphasis on specific learned skills, routines, tasks, degrees, and so on. By learning to look deeper than your skills and experience to the qualities that you bring to a situation—to the creative aspects of your internal strength—you can free yourself from such traps.

Job Search Principle to Follow

Personal qualities are as important as learned skills in making your way in the work world.

All too frequently job descriptions or CVs emphasize only the practical and "recognized" skills, courses, and degrees. Deeper than these acquired assets are inherent qualities like persistence, creativity, loyalty, integrity, and the ability to learn and change that make a major difference in performing effectively.

Your personal motivation and deeper qualities can be the base on which to build a unique and constantly growing variety of skills and capabilities that will prove highly marketable in a changing and demanding work environment.

Strategic Actions

☞ Take three or four people you consider to be successful, in your field or another, and look at the personal qualities they exemplify. With which of these qualities do you identify? Which could you strengthen?

☞ Consider the challenges that arise in your chosen industry or field, ideas that are shaping its future. Think of the qualities that are necessary to successfully meet those challenges.

☞ Use the next exercise to help determine your most marketable personal qualities. Construct a statement around each quality that you could use to impress a prospective employer.

✍ Exercise 6: TOP PERSONAL QUALITIES

Review the following list of personal qualities. Check those that apply to you.

I consider myself to be:

_____ Adaptable	_____ Insightful	_____ Versatile
_____ Willing	_____ Assertive	_____ Perceptive
_____ Thorough	_____ Sensitive	_____ Imaginative
_____ Precise	_____ Productive	_____ Efficient

—— Caring	—— Trustworthy	—— Diligent
—— Honest	—— Helpful	—— Intelligent
—— Hardworking	—— Intuitive	—— Communicative
—— Courageous	—— Strong	—— Determined
—— Dedicated	—— Analytic	—— Committed
—— Forthright	—— Organized	—— Intellectual
—— Tenacious	—— Incisive	—— Persuasive
—— Responsible	—— Warm	—— Flexible
—— Persistent	—— Friendly	—— Humorous

Add more here:

_____   _____   _____

_____   _____   _____

_____   _____   _____

List the four most marketable of these qualities.

1. _____

2. _____

3. _____

4. _____

1.4 TARGETING YOUR FUTURE

SITUATION

Two people are looking for work. The first says she is open to "anything that comes along" and applies for just about every job that appears in the want-ads, sending out dozens of CVs and cover letters each week. Even though she gets a lot of rejections, she also gets called in for quite a few interviews each week. Most, however, are for jobs that neither suit nor interest her. She ends each week thinking that she has accomplished a lot and is ready to follow the same pattern the next week.

The second job seeker follows a different strategy. She targets three specific jobs that she wants to do. She researches which employers in her community can use people for those jobs and focuses her efforts on reaching those employers. She does not get called in for a lot of interviews, but she does have a few quality conversations with potential employers that lead to two job offers.

Working hard to ferret out every job lead is not always the best strategy.

A better approach is to target the jobs that will bring you satisfaction *and* take advantage of your most significant skills and abilities. By focusing your efforts, you will make the best use of your time and, surprisingly, increase your chances of finding meaningful employment quickly.

JOB SEARCH PRINCIPLE TO FOLLOW

A good job target is a work direction that combines your personal interests with your skills.

Once you have a clear job target it is possible to expend energy effectively in pursuit of that target. Without a target, a job search can become aimless and its results unsatisfying.

STRATEGIC ACTIONS

☞ Think of a field of work that would be brand new for you, one that you might have dreamed about becoming involved in, but never thought possible. Find and read a magazine or book about this field and, from this reading, uncover four or five job targets you might be willing to consider.

☞ Think of someone you know who is in a job you feel would be ideally suited to you. What is that job? What would be the next job you would want to have as a step toward that ultimate job?

☞ Ask another person for ideas about possible job targets. A relative or friend can often suggest possibilities that are not apparent to you.

☞ Go to the library and look through help-wanted ads in several papers from other locations. Explore a variety of job titles and list those that could appeal to you.

✍ Exercise 7: JOB POSSIBILITIES

Copy your top five skills and top five interests from Exercises 3 and 4.

Top Five Skills	Top Five Interests
_____	_____
_____	_____
_____	_____
_____	_____
_____	_____

Use your imagination to combine skills and interests to suggest interesting job possibilities. For example, an *interest* in modern dance and a *skill* in computer programming may suggest a position using computers to help choreographers plan new dance techniques.

Skill	/	Interest	Job Possibilities

1. _____/_____   Job 1 _____
                                       Job 2 _____
                                       Job 3 _____
2. _____/_____   Job 1 _____
                                       Job 2 _____
                                       Job 3 _____
3. _____/_____   Job 1 _____
                                       Job 2 _____
                                       Job 3 _____
4. _____/_____   Job 1 _____
                                       Job 2 _____
                                       Job 3 _____
5. _____/_____   Job 1 _____
                                       Job 2 _____
                                       Job 3 _____

Consider your list of job possibilities, along with any other jobs that stimulate your imagination, and narrow the list down to your top five job targets:

Job Targets:

1. _____
2. _____
3. _____
4. _____
5. _____

$\boxed{1.5}$ THE WORLD OF POSSIBILITIES

SITUATION

You've heard that unemployment rates are high, that many employers are thinning their ranks, that automation and computerization are displacing workers at all levels, and that the only jobs available are highly technical or low-paying service positions.

Contrary to popular belief, today's work world has created an unheard-of wealth of job possibilities, many of which did not exist a decade ago. Something like a million new jobs are created a year, in addition to those from the day-to-day turnover of already existing jobs.

You can choose to listen to the pessimists and put your quest for an ideal job on hold until better times, or you can open your eyes to the wealth of undisclosed opportunity that is available in your community. New challenges that business and society must confront demand the creation of new jobs every day. Find a new problem to solve and you will find an opportunity to create a new job.

JOB SEARCH PRINCIPLE TO FOLLOW

A job is an opportunity to solve a problem, and since there is no shortage of problems, there is no shortage of job opportunities.

Most people think of jobs as slots to be filled. They conduct their job search by waiting in line until a slot is vacant on the chance or hope that they will be the next person to fall into the slot.

But there are always new problems to solve and opportunities to seize. New jobs are created all the time to meet the demands, challenges, and opportunities of the moment.

Solving problems is at the heart of the entrepreneurial spirit that has made our economy as dynamic as it is. If you see yourself as a problem solver—or a *career entrepreneur*—you vastly expand the potential market for your skills and capabilities.

STRATEGIC ACTIONS

☞ Consider the following products: a patch on a person's arm which, by administering an ever-smaller dosage of a chemical that makes it possible for the heaviest chain smoker to break the habit; a film package that doubles as a disposable camera; a telephone number that "follows you" no matter where you go; an annuity that guarantees your son or daughter's tuition in ten years; a teleshopping service that enables you to order your groceries for home delivery in two hours. These are only a few of hundreds of products or services that didn't exist a decade ago. List two or three examples from within your job target field. What implications does the creation of these products or services have for your next job target?

☞ People get boxed in by their opinions, beliefs, assumptions, and old habits. From inside these boxes it is very hard to see new developments and the new ways of working that they require. What are some areas in which you may be stuck in old assumptions or beliefs about yourself, your industry, the economy, or your future? List these and challenge them.

☞ List two things you could do that would enable you to expand your thinking about future job opportunities for yourself.

✍ Exercise 8: THE PROBLEM SOLVER

Shift your thinking from the *tasks* that you would do on a job to the *problems* that you could solve. Select three top-priority job targets from the end of Exercise 7 and write them in the appropriate spaces below.

For each job target, identify a problem that you could help solve. It doesn't have to be a complicated problem. The following list may help start you thinking about some common problems:

Cut costs	Improve	Get it done more quickly
Increase sales	Expand	Reduce
Speed up	Get support from	Meet deadlines
Reduce downtime	Organize	

Job target:_____

  Problem to solve:_____

  _____

  _____

Job target:_____

  Problem to solve:_____

  _____

  _____

Job target:_____

  Problem to solve:_____

  _____

  _____

1.6 | THE UNIVERSAL HIRING RULE

SITUATION

You've had a number of interviews and still no job offers. You're becoming a little emotional; thoughts of survival and poverty haunt you. You know that you deserve a job—after all, you've had all those years of studying and work experience. You've really tried hard on this job campaign, and the truth is that you're starting to get a little desperate and angry.

What does it take to convince employers that you are worthy of the chance they need to take?

JOB SEARCH PRINCIPLE TO FOLLOW

The Universal Hiring Rule: Any employer will hire any individual as long as the employer is convinced that the hiring will bring more value than it costs.

The key to career success is the creation of value in the eyes of potential employers. This ability to generate valuable solutions and capitalize on opportunities is what opens doors and breaks down barriers in the job search. By creating and communicating value, you achieve mobility, good job benefits, and the opportunity to choose among numerous possibilities.

This problem-solving approach is not simply that of listing degrees and courses studied; it also embodies performance and contribution. It requires the ability to look afresh at old problems and come up with new ways of thinking and working.

STRATEGIC ACTIONS

☞ Recall and list three things you've done that have produced tangible, quantifiable value.

☞ Consider yourself hired for your next job target. Ask yourself, "Who are the customers? What can I do in this job that will contribute to the value experienced by customers? Who are the others working within the organization? How can my job benefit them?"

☞ Complete the value creation exercise that follows. Use a similar procedure prior to every job interview.

✍ Exercise 9: VALUE CREATION

From Exercise 8, summarize in a few words each of the three problems you identified. Write these summaries on the Problem Statement lines below.

For each Problem Statement, describe the value that could be created by solving the problem. Be specific and try to quantify the value wherever possible.

Next describe the costs—what it takes to create the value. This could be in terms of money, time, resources, materials, energy, stress, and so on.

Problem Statement 1: _____

Value created: _____

_____

Costs: _____

_____

Problem Statement 2: _____

Value created: _____

_____

Costs: _____

_____

Problem Statement 3: _____

Value created: _____

_____

Costs: _____

_____

Go back and review the Universal Hiring Rule. Does the value of your contributions exceed the costs? If not, look for ways to significantly increase the value.

1.7 LIFETIME LEARNING AND DEVELOPMENT

SITUATION

You are caught in a dilemma. You need to be a specialist to get a good job, but as a specialist you run the risk of your skills becoming obsolete as new technologies replace old ones. Should you stand on the knowledge foundation you've already built or . . .

Job Search Principle to Follow

Capability development leads to career development. By constantly enhancing your skills and your ability to deliver results, you enhance your versatility and the scope of your career as well as your earning potential.

In today's career marketplace it is essential to continue to develop and learn. Lifelong learning and personal development are important aspects in achieving career success and satisfaction. Changing technologies, markets, and global needs require that you continually expand your scope of knowledge, skills, and capabilities. Careers no longer run on rails that you can get on at one location and proceed directly to a stop up the line. Careers have become more a composite of changes influenced by shifts in external demands along with internal personal growth and development. The straight-line career has now become a journey on which you change tracks to go off in different directions or change modes of transportation altogether.

Strategic Actions

☞ Think of a recent work or study assignment. What challenges did this assignment pose to your understanding or knowledge of a particular task, technology, or procedure? What could you learn that would expand your knowledge or capability in this area?

☞ Think of somebody who is a few steps ahead of you in your career path or direction. What could you learn from a conversation or series of conversations with that person? Are you willing to have such a conversation?

☞ Search out publications in your job target field. Take the time to read these publications. Look for new areas of study that you believe would make you more marketable.

☞ Use the capability development exercise that follows to target a personal development plan.

✍ Exercise 10: CAPABILITY DEVELOPMENT

Capabilities exist beyond the requirements of any specific job. By building your base of capabilities, you increase your potential to achieve new levels of satisfaction and performance in the future.

Think about your job targets. Ask yourself what areas of capability you need to develop or improve to produce better results and gain a greater sense of satisfaction from the job.

Complete the following capability statements that express *what* you want to develop, *how* you will use your inner qualities in that development, and what *results* you want to produce.

I want to increase my proficiency in _using a computer spreadsheet_
by _spending scheduled time with Bill_
so that _I can be a better financial planner._

I want to increase my proficiency in_____
(What area, skill, or ability do I want to develop?)
by_____
(How do I want to do this?)
so that_____
(What do I want as a result of developing this capability?)
What actions can I take to attain this goal?_____
_____
_____
_____

By when do I want to complete this goal?_____

I want to increase my proficiency in_____
(What area, skill, or ability do I want to develop?)
by_____
(How do I want to do this?)
so that_____
(What do I want as a result of developing this capability?)
What actions can I take to attain this goal?_____
_____
_____
_____

By when do I want to complete this goal?_____

I want to increase my proficiency in_____
(What area, skill, or ability do I want to develop?)
by_____
(How do I want to do this?)
so that_____
(What do I want as a result of developing this capability?)
What actions can I take to attain this goal?_____
_____
_____
_____

By when do I want to complete this goal?_____

1.8 Creating Security Through Versatility

SITUATION

You've invested a lot in your education, in on-the-job training, and in your personal experience. You've become well known for your skills and your specialization. Yet market changes have you worried: You've heard of layoffs from similar positions in other organizations. When you started your career, your path seemed secure and limitless, but now it feels shaky. You know that it is important to maintain your financial security and your marketability. You're concerned about how to hold on to what you've got.

JOB SEARCH PRINCIPLE TO FOLLOW

Versatility is a prerequisite for personal security in the work environment of the nineties.

Job security is a myth. External changes in the market, corporate shake-ups, economic influences, and growth in technology have caused massive restructuring of organizations with consequent layoffs, resizing, early retirements, and loss of work for hundreds of thousands. To depend on one job to produce continuity and security is a mistake. Versatility and the ability to deal with the new and the different in a positive way are the qualities that generate the truest potential for internal security and well-being.

STRATEGIC ACTIONS

☞ Consider your industry or field as a whole. Talk to people who are familiar with the larger picture and get their ideas about what's changing, what competitors are doing, what new technologies are being introduced.

☞ Take some time to examine how the functions you are performing or have performed can be integrated with other functions in your organization so that your job becomes larger. How do you get closer to the customer? How can you relate to suppliers and vendors? How do you integrate your work into other departments? Given these possibilities, what qualities do you need to develop in yourself to extend beyond the limits of your specific job?

✍ **Exercise 11: PERFORMANCE QUALITIES**

Performance qualities are ways of working that enhance your ability to execute a job. Check the performance qualities that represent your strengths.

_____ Have a good understanding of business

_____ Make valuable suggestions

_____ Concentrate on getting the job done

_____ Put strong emphasis on quality results

_____ Follow procedures accurately

_____ Exhibit leadership ability

_____ Take care of equipment and property

_____ Show loyalty

_____ Take risks

_____ Communicate clearly

_____ Maintain positive energy

_____ Maintain self-discipline

_____ Work effectively under pressure

_____ Concentrate in spite of distractions

_____ Demonstrate versatility

_____ Understand how profits are created

_____ Perform well in emergencies

_____ Show initiative

_____ Analyze complex problems

_____ Make efficient use of time

_____ Work effectively on a team

_____ Train people well

_____ Energize and motivate others

_____ Accept changes easily

_____ Adapt to new conditions

_____ Rise to new challenges

_____ Show good workmanship

_____ Accept criticism

_____ Plan well

_____ Perform physically difficult work

_____ Challenge old ways of thinking

_____ Manifest high personal standards

1.9 NEW WAYS OF WORKING

SITUATION

You decided that 9-to-5 job duty is just not for you. Real life has turned out to be more multifaceted than you expected, and you want to spend more time with your growing family, in your community, or on your outside interests. You know that you are marketable and that it would be no problem to get another job. However, you don't want just another job. You want your life to expand to include more home and noncareer pursuits. You're anxious to remodel your work agreements and practices.

JOB SEARCH PRINCIPLE TO FOLLOW

In today's work world it is possible to shape the job you want in many more dimensions than simply those of title, hours, and compensation.

The diversity of work, aided by technology and rapid changes in jobs requirements, allows you to select from a variety of work styles: It is possible to work at home, part-time, freelance, or as a consultant and still achieve a satisfying income. By exploring different work styles and opportunities you can tailor your work situations to family needs and personal development objectives.

STRATEGIC ACTIONS

☞ Find some people in your industry or field who work freelance or as consultants. Meet with them and find out how they do it, what they've learned, and what the problems and pitfalls are.

☞ Analyze your most recent job, making a list of what tasks need to be done at the employer's location and what could be done elsewhere.

☞ Go to the library and read current publications concerned with running a home office, starting your own business, and so on. Seek out others who are choosing work styles similar to yours and/or who may have written articles about their experiences. Call them up to find out what the drawbacks are and how they go about negotiating their work assignments.

☞ Use Exercise 12 to design a potential scenario that will satisfy your quest for a more imaginative way to live and work.

☞ When you have completed Exercise 12, think of how to present your ideas to your current or future employer in a way that demonstrates how your proposal would be valuable to her as well as to you. This thinking will be useful in developing your CV and in preparing for interviews.

✍ Exercise 12: WORK STYLES

Take a few moments for yourself. Don't think about specific jobs or employers. This is your time to indulge your imagination *and* be truthful with yourself. Don't worry about what you think is "supposed" to be or what others have said that you "should" do.

Ask yourself what role or values you want your career to provide in your life. Consider the following items and check any statement that applies to you.

_____ I want to train myself to become very qualified and skilled in a professional field.

_____ I derive most of my identity and purpose in life from the work I do.

_____ I am committed to the organization I work for and want to think that that organization relies on my talents to succeed.

_____ I am willing to work hard for promotions and recognition.

_____ I want a full-time, secure position and am willing to put in forty or more hours per week, often working evenings or weekends if necessary.

_____ I am willing to accept that a large part of my salary is based on my performance or the performance of the organization.

_____ I am willing to work hard and for long hours in return for a strong possibility of future promotion.

_____ I am willing to give my job my best, but I don't want it to interfere with my family life.

_____ I do not want a demanding job and would rather put my energy into other areas of my life.

_____ I am committed to my work but want to leave it at the end of a normal workday.

_____ I am interested in part-time, seasonal, or short-term employment.

_____ I want to be paid for the hours that I put in whether or not the organization is profitable.

_____ I am interested in being a consultant and wouldn't mind working for others (short- or long-term) who need my talents.

_____ I prefer to work for myself rather than an organization.

_____ If I am working for someone else, I want to be able to take off periods of time and know that work is there for me when I return.

_____ I want to be paid well for the results that I produce and can tolerate periods of unemployment.

_____ I want the freedom to set my own hours and working conditions.

_____ I want to work out of my home, communicating with my employer through technology (phone, fax, computer).

_____ Other work styles I prefer:

_____ _____

_____ _____

_____ _____

_____ _____

_____ _____

Using the statements that you checked, think about what type of work style you want as part of your life. Describe the following elements of your newly defined work style:

The type of organization:_____
_____

Your work setting:_____
_____

Your work schedule:_____
_____

How you receive payment for the work you do:_____
_____

The type of training you need to do your job:_____
_____

The type of people with whom you work:_____
_____

A typical day at your job:_____
_____
_____

1.10 THE JOB THAT KEEPS ON WORKING FOR YOU

SITUATION

Your day-to-day routine has lost its flavor, and there's an empty feeling in your stomach when you head off to work each morning. The adventure and challenge of the job has worn thin for you, and there's not much to compensate for their loss. Salary isn't a problem, and your competency on the job is not at issue. What is at issue is personal satisfaction, growth, and a sense of meaning.

JOB SEARCH PRINCIPLE TO FOLLOW

The ideal job is the job that keeps on working for you.

When you are engaged in productive activities whose source is your inherent self-esteem and capability, you are rewarded with a satisfaction that fills your spirit as well as your wallet. By looking deeply beneath the surface of the job market for those opportunities that really resonate with your sense of self, you can create powerful possibilities for growth and development.

STRATEGIC ACTIONS

☞ List five things that you don't like about work.

☞ List five things that could excite you about work—in your current job or another.

☞ List the names of four people whose work you respect (either living or in history).

✎ Exercise 13: A QUALITY WORK LIFE

Create a vision of what a quality work life looks like to you. Start by asking yourself the following questions:

Imagine an ideal job for which you look forward to getting up in the morning and getting right to work. What does it look like?_____

_____

Imagine an ideal job in which you know you are accomplishing something useful for others. What does it look like?_____

_____

Imagine an ideal job in which you have all the resources you need to get the job done. What does it look like?_____

_____

Imagine an ideal job in which you are fully appreciated for what you do. What does it look like?_____

_____

Imagine an ideal job that is an exciting adventure for you. What does it look like?_____

_____

Imagine an ideal job in which you are excited by what you are learning so that you want to learn more and more. What does it look like?_____

_____

Use the following space to draw a diagram or picture of your vision of a high-quality work life. Show as many elements as possible. The quality of this drawing itself is not important; it's the creative thinking that counts.

My Career Vision

[Use objects, symbols, words, or other graphics to demonstrate visually what a high-quality work life looks like to you.]

1.11 THINK GLOBALLY

SITUATION

As an observer of our current world, you see enormous changes taking place: political disintegration and revitalization, economic restructuring, an explosion of growth in technology, and so forth. You long to be part of this expanding, dynamic landscape, but your job seems mundane and routine. You wonder whether your role is to be an observer of change or an enthusiastic participant.

JOB SEARCH PRINCIPLE TO FOLLOW

The job market is global, multicultural, and multifaceted.

A stable job in a stable industry in a familiar geography can be a persuasive trap. We are entering a truly global work environment. Today's job market is expanding geographically and embracing new cultural and technical languages. Those who succeed are those who stretch their imaginations beyond their hometowns to more distant places on the planet and to more varied opportunities within the economy. Mobility, versatility, and the ability to deal with change and uncertainty are key characteristics of the successful job seeker and career entrepreneur.

STRATEGIC ACTIONS

☞ Reach out and meet people of other disciplines, cultures, and nationalities. Talk to them about what is happening in their world. Go beyond the superficial and learn what's really happening.

☞ On your next vacation, take a trip to a remote location that you've never before thought of visiting, someplace known for its dynamic growth and change. This might be Eastern Europe, Germany, Japan, or Southern California. On your trip do more than simply check out the scenery. See if you can meet people who live there or visit a professional association or organization. Contact the chamber of commerce for information about what is going on in the area and seek out people in a similar field to yours.

☞ If you don't know how to use a computer, take the time to learn. Explore this technology beyond its games and simple word processing, into the realm of communications, strategic planning, and personal development.

☞ Look for ways that your own department or organization can become more multicultural and diverse.

1.12 Breaking Out of Boxes

Situation

Your instincts tell you what to do and how to conduct your job search. You know the rules of the game. The actions you take and the paths you follow are consistent with these rules.

Actions you choose to take are, for the most part, comfortable for you. Why should you do anything that puts you out on a limb, involves risk, or makes you slightly uncomfortable?

Are you being boxed in by the approaches that you have assumed to be best? Could you be missing out on great opportunities that otherwise could be yours?

Job Search Principle to Follow

A truly creative job search takes courage, the willingness to challenge that which is familiar, and the desire to enter a new world of possibility.

In the formal job search, you can get boxed in by past experiences, old mental models, and old assumptions, beliefs, and opinions. It is possible to challenge the assumptions, the educational requirements, and the other demands of the want-ads.

To be a true career entrepreneur you must break out of old boundaries and create new opportunities by communicating with prospective employers in a way that expands their thinking and creates new work situations. This approach is new and unconventional; but in fact it is exactly the direction in which business is headed—toward innovation, challenge, opportunity, and the creation of new ways of working.

Strategic Actions

☞ What assumptions have you made about yourself, your capability, and your potential that could be boxing you in from realizing your fullest potential?

☞ What have you taken for granted about your capabilities, what limits have you imposed on yourself?

☞ What fears block you from creating a work experience or career direction that could be more exciting and challenging? List these fears.

✍ Exercise 14: BREAK OUT OF BOXES

Pay attention to the assumptions that you make about career opportunities in your field, your specific job search, your limitations, or any other preconceptions that could possibly limit your point of view. For example: "There are no jobs in my field" or "I never went to college—no one would give me a salary of £35,000."

Use this exercise to help you move forward by breaking old assumptions, beliefs, and opinions.

List one (or more) assumption(s) that may box you in to a limited view of yourself:

_____

_____

_____

_____

_____

What are some more positive assumptions to operate from?

_____

_____

_____

_____

What actions can you take to reinforce the more positive view?_____

_____

_____

_____

1.13 IT'S UP TO YOU

SITUATION

You find yourself blaming the economy, the employers who have just merged to eliminate your job, the lack of vision in people who have interviewed you, and your mother and father for not having left you a bigger nest egg. All those factors point to a bleak future. How do you break out of this narrow perspective?

JOB SEARCH PRINCIPLE TO FOLLOW

You are responsible for the quality of your work life.

Many of us labor under the assumptions that employers and education are responsible for directing us to careers that are satisfying and stable. Unfortunately, this is no longer true. You must take responsibility for developing your own job plan and orchestrating your own job and career searches.

Responsibility is scary. On the one hand, personal responsibility takes away the pretense that our education, degrees, and gilt-edged job history guarantee our future. On the positive side, a sense of responsibility for and commitment to your own future allows you to initiate action, to go beyond old job titles to meet changing interests, and to develop and market your potential to its maximum.

STRATEGIC ACTION

☞ Make an honest list of those forces, people, or events that you blame for your current condition.

✍ Exercise 15: SUCCESS AFFIRMATION

Accepting responsibility and focusing your thinking on success can be a difficult process. Old opinions, beliefs, doubts, and assumptions can undermine your will to succeed. A powerful method for directing subconscious thinking is to consciously affirm your belief that you can succeed.

Affirmations are statements that accentuate the positive in a way that reflects the progress you want to make.

EXAMPLES

- I am responsible for the quality of my work life.
- I can create value for others and satisfaction for myself.
- I can combine my interests in music with my skills in marketing to create an ideal job.

Write down five affirmations of your own:

- I _____
- I _____
- I _____
- I _____
- I _____

References

The Career Discovery Project Gerald Sturman (Aurum)

What Color Is Your Parachute? Richard N. Bolles (Ten Speed Press)

A Whack on the Side of the Head Roger Van Oech (Thorsons)

The Age of Unreason Charles Handy (Century)

How to Find the Perfect Job Tom Jackson (Piatkus)

Which Way Now? Bridget Wright (Piatkus)

Changing Course Maggie Smith (Mercury)

Career Turnaround Viney/Jones (Thorsons)

Changing Your Job After 35 Godfrey Golzen (Kogan Page)

Build Your Own Rainbow Hopson/Scully (Mercury)

Smart Moves Golzen/Garner (Blackwell)

10 Steps to the Top Marie Jennings (Piatkus)

Getting on the Fast Track: Jumping Hurdles to Success

Once you have a purpose and vision for your job search, the obstacles will start showing up. You discover very quickly that it is not necessarily the most qualified people that get the best jobs; it is frequently those most skilled in the art and strategies of job finding. The task of getting the best job for yourself is a job in itself. It takes work and persistence as well as imagination, courage, and creativity. Barriers can be expected and can be cleared—just like hurdles at a high-performance track and field event.

It is important to remember throughout your job search that you and the employer are equal parties in a negotiation. You're not a supplicant with hat in hand. You are a dynamic, value-laden prospect that the employer wants and needs to fill a very vital role in his or her organization.

A strong support system is essential to keep your career in fast play—people who can give you feedback, ideas, and suggestions, who can help you to stick to your schedule, encourage you when you're feeling low, and acknowledge your successes and victories. The strategies suggested in this book take some doing, and they work much better when you're supported by others. We invite you to have a partner in your journey.

We stress the need for action—action with creativity and innovation. It's all too easy to theorize and fantasize and then forget to make that important phone call, forget to take action. Worries and doubts (about recession, unemployment, and scarcity of opportunities) can demoralize you if you don't take intelligent action. So it's important to be truthful with yourself about the barriers and blocks that get in your way and, in working with this book and your support system, to identify the actions that will clear your path.

Job Search Principles

2.1 It's not the most qualified people who get the best jobs; it's those who are most skilled at job finding.

2.2 Getting the perfect job is a job in itself.

2.3 Barriers are to be anticipated.

2.4 You and the employer are equal parties.

2.5 A support system is essential for success.

2.6 Try something new.

2.7 Action works.

2.8 Don't believe in recessions.

2.9 Don't depend on the want-ads.

2.10 Pay attention to your psychology.

2.1 BEING SKILLED AT JOB FINDING

SITUATION

You've done well in your career so far. You've achieved good performance reviews, continued your training and education, developed confidence in your capabilities to get things done. But now you're faced with a career change. At first you thought it would be easy: You tell a few friends who will pass the word along that you're in the job market. Since you're skilled and able, you're sure to hear about something in a week or two. You wait . . . time passes . . . No one's knocking on the door or ringing the phone off the hook, so you put out a little more bait, let more people know. Now you're alarmed. Why aren't companies leaping at the opportunity to bring you on board? You're clearly qualified, and yet—you're not quite sure what you should do to sell yourself in a competitive market. It's time to learn a new set of skills—the skills of the perfect job search.

JOB SEARCH PRINCIPLE TO FOLLOW

It's not the most qualified people who get the best jobs; it's those who are most skilled at job finding.

Most of our education loads us with information and skills but very few ideas about how to put them to work. All payload and no delivery system.

You may freeze when faced with the need to be proactive in creating your future. You may not be accustomed to taking the initiative in your career, although this is one of the most important capabilities you can develop for yourself.

Learn the skills of a self-directed, responsible job search. Exercise your will and courage to find new pathways in the hidden job market. Don't wait for opportunity to knock. You may have to break the door down.

STRATEGIC ACTIONS

✍ Exercise 16: JOB SEARCH SKILLS INVENTORY

Review the list of job search strategies and techniques listed here. These are critical actions that will contribute significantly to the success of your search for a meaningful and satisfying job.

In each of the following, rate yourself on a scale from least proficient (1) to most proficient (10).

	1 (Poor)	5 (OK)	10 (Great)
	|–+–+–+–+–|–+–+–+–+–|		
• Analyzing my skills, interests, and personal qualities to expand my thinking about possible job areas. (1.2)	|–+–+–+–+–|–+–+–+–+–|		
• Identifying a clearly defined job target. (1.4).	|–+–+–+–+–|–+–+–+–+–|		
• Honestly looking at barriers that might be in the way of conducting an effective job search. (2.3)	|–+–+–+–+–|–+–+–+–+–|		
• Contacting at least fifteen people—friends, relatives, associates—to create an effective support system. (2.5)	|–+–+–+–+–|–+–+–+–+–|		
• Preparing an effective, accomplishments-oriented CV (4.2)	|–+–+–+–+–|–+–+–+–+–|		
• Researching potential employers using the library and other resources. (3.3)	|–+–+–+–+–|–+–+–+–+–|		
• Creating hard-hitting, custom cover letters. (5.1)	|–+–+–+–+–|–+–+–+–+–|		

- Making numerous phone calls to individuals, associates, and organizations to obtain information about potential employers. (3.6). . . . . |−+−+−+−+−|−+−+−+−+−|
- Telephoning specific hiring-level managers and supervisors to set up interview appointments. (6.2). . . . . |−+−+−+−+−|−+−+−+−+−|
- Preparing for interviews by conducting research and putting together an effective presentation. (7.2) . . . . |−+−+−+−+−|−+−+−+−+−|
- Practicing interviews before they take place. (7.14) . . . . |−+−+−+−+−|−+−+−+−+−|
- Making follow-up phone calls or writing thank-you letters to everyone whom I have contacted regarding my job search. (8.2) . . . . |−+−+−+−+−|−+−+−+−+−|
- Actively seeking feedback on how I communicate. (8.3) . . . . |−+−+−+−+−|−+−+−+−+−|
- Setting and meeting specific deadlines for accomplishing goals. (2.2). . . . . |−+−+−+−+−|−+−+−+−+−|
- Negotiating for my desired salary and benefits. (9.4) . . . . |−+−+−+−+−|−+−+−+−+−|
- Evaluating job offers to be sure that they meet my desired level of work satisfaction. (9.1). . . . . |−+−+−+−+−|−+−+−+−+−|

The gaps between where you are today and where you would like to be as a high-performing, active, effective job seeker clearly show which areas need your closest attention. The number after each statement in this exercise directs you to the section in this book that addresses that specific activity. Do a scan of what you need to know to make the most of your current job search challenge and set aside time to read the material and then draw up an action plan.

2.2 IT'S A JOB TO FIND A JOB

SITUATION

You *have* worked at it. You've let people know you're available. You've spent a couple of days on your CV. You've connected with headhunters. And with all that, not much has happened. Time is passing, you're getting discouraged, and yet you have a vague sense that perhaps you're not doing enough. You resent the fact that people aren't more responsive to you and that you've got to take even more initiative.

Job Search Principle to Follow

Getting the perfect job is a job in itself.

It takes an organized work plan and strategy to get the kind of work you want. It takes initiative, imagination, and focused energy. It's important to practice your skills, to read more than one book, to role-play, and to follow the necessary steps in your self-directed job search. You've got to know what you want to do and how to go about doing it.

Strategic Actions

☞ Get yourself a calendar and a portable organizer at any stationery store. If you are employed, set aside an appropriate number (minimum 3 per month if you're serious about it) of half days for "personal work." If you're unemployed or just getting started in your search, set aside larger blocks of time, perhaps four five-hour periods per week. Use this time solely for concentrating on your job search.

☞ Schedule some personal time for recreation, rehabilitation, and activities with family and friends. Don't overdo your job search. Plan it strategically.

✍ Exercise 17: TIMELINE

Estimate on the timeline given below the time you think it will take to work through each step of the job search process and to reach your ultimate goal. You can do the timeline in one of two ways:

1. Beginning at the top of the chart (the visionary approach), set your goal for the date by which you plan to have a new job. Working from the top down, and giving a full measure of time to each stage, fill in the dates by which you should complete each step toward that goal. Once you work out the time for each step, you may have to adjust the date of your ultimate goal.

2. Beginning at the bottom of the chart (the logical approach), estimate how long each step of the process will take, beginning today, and fill in an appropriate date on which you should have each step completed. If the date for your ultimate goal turns out to be too far in the future, see if you can condense some of the intervals between steps.

Targeted
Completion Date   *Job Search Benchmarks*

_____   Accept job offer.

_____   Negotiate terms.

_____   Receive job offers.

——— ———	Conduct interviews.
————————	Practice for interviews.
————————	Set up interviews with prospective employers.
————————	Make contacts to locate the decision maker for each targeted employer.
————————	Prepare CVs, cover letters, and supporting materials tailored to the targeted employers.
————————	Finalize a list of targeted employers.
————————	Research prospective employers.
————————	Identify a clear job target.
————————	Analyze personal interests to expand my thinking about possible job areas.

☞ Since this book is about getting what you want in your work life, it is important for you to look at your goals. To achieve a goal, you must start with a clear objective in mind. Many people confuse goals with a vague future hope. Or they set lofty goals for themselves without the intention to realize them. Goals should be a measure of what you can attain, not just what you hope. Your hopes and dreams are important in creating vision and direction for yourself. Your goals are specific locations in space and time that you can achieve.

There are three criteria for an effective goal:

- It is specific: Know what it is you want to happen.
- It is measurable: Quantify it.
- It is determinable by you: You have full control over achieving it.

Examples:

"My goal is to get a good job and make a lot of money." This is not a goal. It's not specific and measurable.

"My goal is to secure a job as a graphics programmer with an annual salary of £50,000 for a company that creates software games." This is a clearer goal in that it is more specific and measurable, but it is not determinable by you. You are not in complete control.

"My goal is to make ten phone calls to software companies that create games." This goal is specific (phone calls), measurable (ten), and in your control. It is up to you, not someone else, whether the phone calls get made or not.

The importance of setting goals is that you can actually measure your progress, not your frustrations. Keep your goals simple. Establish a goal for even the most basic activity that you do on a regular basis. Do not set goals that you cannot accomplish.

✍ Exercise 18: GOAL SETTING

As you begin your work for each block of time set aside for your job search, take a few minutes to set your goals each day. Write down three to five specific, attainable goals. You are more likely to attain these goals if you write them down. Use the following format or the Daily Log on page 138.

Goal Statement

A goal I want to accomplish (today):_____

_____

Actions to complete this goal:_____

_____

_____

_____

I will know I have successfully completed this goal when_____

_____

Schedule your time: A daily or weekly schedule is a valuable tool for managing your time. It reminds you of appointments and commitments; it forces you to set aside time to work on your goals. A schedule disciplines you to make full use of your time and to treat job seeking as a high priority. Here are some guidelines to help you develop a schedule:

1. Start by writing down all of your planned appointments.

2. Reserve some time at the beginning of the day to organize yourself. Take time to plan your goals for the day, review your schedule, gather any materials you need, and think strategically about the best use of your time.

3. Reserve time to review and update your contact lists. Keep a card or computer file of everyone in your contact network (see Sections 2.5 and 3.5). As part of your planning process for the day, review this file, make notes, and add names of new contacts. Make a list of anyone you have not recently contacted.

4. Take time in the morning to look up job leads, contact employers by phone, or work on CVs and cover letters. Devote your afternoons and early evenings to personal contacts, interviews, and meetings.

5. Take time at the end of each day to review and evaluate your accomplishments. Did you do everything you wanted to do? What did you put off doing? What happened that was unexpected? Make short notes on how you did.

6. Plan some time for planning the next day and next week. What new goals do you want to introduce?

7. Schedule time for leisure activities. Take breaks. You need time to relax and time to build new competences. Use every moment to your advantage. It's OK to have some fun.

2.3 BARRIERS AND HURDLES ARE TO BE ANTICIPATED

SITUATION

You've worked hard at your job search and are getting frustrated. Your rejection rate is too high; employers aren't returning your calls; interviews aren't leading to offers. You start to lose confidence in the organized process of a self-directed job search. You've run into the inevitable barriers and blocks, disappointments, objections, and difficulties. You want to stop.

JOB SEARCH PRINCIPLE TO FOLLOW

Barriers are to be anticipated.

You won't meet resistance until you push forward. The tip of the spade against the earth produces nothing. It's only when you apply energy that the work gets done.

In managing your career with intention and drive, you will inevitably create resistance. Your work is in overcoming the obstacles blocking your way. Anticipating barriers and hurdles is a normal part of mastering the self-directed job search. To address these barriers consciously and find ways to overcome them is a requirement for forging your own path to success.

STRATEGIC ACTIONS

☞ Keep a list of blocks and disappointments—not to agonize over them, but simply to recognize them. Identify the barrier clearly for what it is, without adding emotional drama to it. If the employer decided to hire someone else, for instance, do not write, "I've been rejected again."

☞ Make the distinction between real barriers and simple excuses. When you find yourself complaining about the economy, the lack of response from employers, the lack of opportunity, and so on, you may be using these as justifications to keep yourself from taking action. This habit of complaining reinforces a lack of responsibility and keeps you from moving ahead. Take another point of view: Since you can't change many of the external circumstances, the only thing you can do is move ahead regardless of them.

✍ Exercise 19: IDENTIFYING BARRIERS

Check everything in the following list that you feel does or could get in the way of your achieving a better job or more satisfying work life.

_____ I don't have enough experience in the field.
_____ I'm too young.
_____ I'm too old.
_____ The economy is weak.
_____ Unemployment is increasing.
_____ I'm overqualified.
_____ They wouldn't hire a woman.
_____ They wouldn't hire a minority.
_____ They wouldn't hire a _____.
_____ There are no jobs.
_____ They can't make up their minds.
_____ My skills are obsolete.
_____ I don't know how to operate a computer.
_____ It's impossible to get interviews.
_____ There are too many applicants chasing each job.
_____ All the jobs are in the suburbs.
_____ All the jobs are in the city.
_____ I don't have the right education.
_____ I have too much education.
_____ They really don't want to hire anyone.
_____ Add others:

_____ _____
_____ _____
_____ _____
_____ _____
_____ _____
_____ _____
_____ _____

At any given moment in your job campaign, it is possible to blame many external reasons for not achieving what you want when you want it. The truth is that your quest for the best job is probably impeded by only one factor: your resistance to doing what's necessary to get the results you want.

The real barriers are generally internal doubts, fears, resistance to change—perfectly normal everyday psychological baggage. The only way to deal with such barriers is first to identify them specifically and then to determine if you are willing to take the steps necessary to overcome them.

✍ Exercise 20: DEEPER BARRIERS

Review the statements you checked in Exercise 19, and then answer each question below as honestly as you can.

1. In your experience, what are your biggest internal blocks in the way of your job search?

_____

_____

_____

2. What is the single most powerful personal barrier or behavior that might stand in the way of your doing what it takes to obtain a job with maximum work satisfaction?

_____

_____

_____

3. What actions can you take to start the process of overcoming the barriers you listed above?

_____

_____

_____

_____

2.4 JOB SEEKING IS A WORTHY ACTIVITY

SITUATION

When your job search comes up against barriers and difficulties, and your good hard work seems unrewarded by employers, you may unconsciously begin to relegate all the power in the situation to the employer. It may seem that others are there only to judge you and that the interviewer controls your future and fortune. Remind yourself that the negotiation between you and the employer is one between equals. You have great value to deliver, and the employer has needs to be met. Operate on the assertion of your value, and you will discover that your relationships with employers will become equal.

JOB SEARCH PRINCIPLE TO FOLLOW

You and the employer are equal parties.

Many of us hold the old notion that jobs are scarce. Jobs are opportunities to solve problems, and there are sufficient problems to keep us all happily and gainfully occupied.

In looking at jobs as scarce you may attribute certain power and authority to employers that they do not possess. The truth is that employers need you as much as you need them. Employers can maintain their organizations only to the degree that they find good people able to perform their jobs in a proficient and value-producing way.

When you start to see yourself and the employer as equal parties in a negotiation, your own self-esteem and potential value become more apparent.

STRATEGIC ACTIONS

☞ Spend time as part of a professional association, a community organization, or an alumni association. Volunteer for as many activities as you can. Seek situations in which you will be with people who are employed and are your peers. Don't drift into the background when you become successful. Stay in the foreground.

☞ List those people with whom you normally work, such as suppliers, customers, colleagues, or professional associates. Think of ways to stay in touch with them, not to complain of your difficulties, but to participate in an ongoing relationship with peers.

☞ Return to Section 1.6, Exercise 9, and review the problems you identified and the value you can create by solving those problems. The only way you are going to see yourself as an equal partner to an employer is to believe in the value you can create for that employer. Employers do not hire out of charity. They have problems that they want to solve.

Exercise 21: SELF-ESTEEM

Review the work you did in Chapter 1 to identify what makes you a unique person. Complete the following sections.

The Value I Offer	*The Value I Expect*
My knowledge of _____ _____ _____ _____	The opportunity to develop and grow in _____ _____ _____
My skills, including my ability to __ _____ _____ _____	Personal satisfaction from _____ _____ _____ _____
The qualities that make me a high performer are: _____ _____ _____	An opportunity to live the lifestyle I want, including an ability to _____ _____ _____
The money results I can produce: __ _____ _____	The money I need: _____ _____ _____
Other assets that I offer: _____ _____ _____ _____	Other possibilities of value that the employer can provide: _____ _____ _____

$\boxed{2.5}$ Build Support Networks

Situation

If you're between jobs, you may start to feel uncomfortable on weekdays when your former workmates are on the job. You may begin telling yourself that you need to get going faster, try new things, be more courageous. You seem to be going around in circles and end up stuck deeper in the very condition you are trying to talk yourself out of. Making a job or career change is not something that you can do well without outside help.

Job Search Principle to Follow

A support system is essential for success.

An emotional shadow and potential for rejection haunt many job searches. You may find it enormously helpful to work with two or three other people to organize and carry out your job search. These people should be collaborators, not critics. They need not be professional career counselors, but rather coaches: friends, family, colleagues, mentors—people who are committed to your success and well-being.

Take the risk of asking for the support you need. Developing reciprocal support among three or four people is an excellent approach. Maintain relationships with supporters who tell you the truth about how to move things ahead. Those who avoid telling you what's going on or who don't want to tell you something unpleasant or "unkind" are not needed right now. The best feedback is that which helps you target what you want.

Strategic Actions

☞ Make a list of those areas in which you would like support: financial planning, role playing, research, networking, problem solving, strategic planning, and so on. Think of one or two people in each category and list them, whether or not you know them personally, if you have even a suspicion that they would be willing to help you. List the names first and then think of ways to meet those people one-on-one. Ask for support, advice, coaching, or referrals to others. Do it. They won't bite.

☞ Set up your own personal support network. People will offer all kinds of support if you ask them. Inform them of your motivation to find meaningful and satisfying work. They can help you research your skills and gather career information; they can provide feedback and critique your interview performance.

Changing jobs or starting a new job should be a time of opportunity, not of fear that the world will end. However, financial problems can cause a great deal of distress. Sometimes this distress can be eliminated. Your personal support system can offer financial support if you approach the subject correctly, with security and motivation.

✍ Exercise 22: YOUR SUPPORT NETWORK

Select as many people as you can from your personal support system of family, relatives, friends, neighbors, clergy, co-workers. Write names and telephone numbers in the spaces here. Below each name, write what that person can do to help your campaign. Call each person to ask for support.

Dates Contacted

Name: _____ Phone: _____
Ways to help: _____
_____

Name: _____ Phone: _____
Ways to help: _____
_____

Name: _____ Phone: _____
Ways to help: _____
_____

Name: _____ Phone: _____
Ways to help: _____
_____

Name: _____ Phone: _____
Ways to help: _____
_____

Name: _____ Phone: _____
Ways to help: _____
_____

Name: _____ Phone: _____				
Ways to help: _____ _____			

Name: _____ Phone: _____				
Ways to help: _____ _____			

Name: _____ Phone: _____				
Ways to help: _____ _____			

Name: _____ Phone: _____				
Ways to help: _____ _____			

2.6 TRY SOMETHING NEW

SITUATION

Your job search seems to be on track: You've targeted right, researched well, communicated regularly and effectively to get interviews. But somehow you're caught in an old cycle: You follow the process, but the results are just mediocre. It's time for a little innovation.

JOB SEARCH PRINCIPLE TO FOLLOW

Try something new.

Traditional job search strategies have become just that—traditional and predictable. To be most effective today, a job search needs an element that's unique. Thousands of people complain about lack of responsiveness from employers, but few assume the responsibility to try something innovative.

Take the initiative. Call people who might not seem to be the obvious contacts; go beyond the personnel office. Try something different even if you are not sure of its outcome. You have nothing to lose.

Remember that hundreds of thousands of employers need problem solvers like you. Experiment with new ways to let them know about you. Without experimentation, you'll be stuck in a long line of candidates seeking to fill a finite number of slots.

STRATEGIC ACTIONS

☞ Get six or seven trade journals in your field, read them, and identify their contributing writers. Find out what you can about the writers, including how to contact them. Call them, and see if you can set up a meeting to learn something.

☞ Look through your high school or college yearbook for faces you still remember. Find out what your old friends are doing. Then call them and ask them for some advice or leads. Most alumni associations maintain an accurate record of where alumni live.

☞ Read the columns in newspapers and journals related to personnel changes and new appointments. Choose a person in an interesting position related to your job search. Wait a week or so until she has settled into her new job and then send a letter offering ways you can help her get off to a fast start.

☞ Enroll in a class related to your field or industry. Do this not only to learn some new things, but also to gain new references and insights. Socialize with your classmates.

☞ Volunteer for civic and professional projects that will bring you in touch with relevant contacts.

☞ If you run out of leads, go to a major office building where you'd like to work and check what companies have offices in that building. You can stop at their offices to find out more about their organizations or ask for annual reports, product information, or even job applications. Don't wait for a job to show up in the help-wanted ads.

☞ Read government publications announcing contract awards and contact people who recently received them. Think of how you can help them fulfill their contracts.

✍ Exercise 23: THE NONTRADITIONAL JOB SEARCH

Here is a list of nontraditional job search activities for you to consider. Each involves some action on your part that will help you stand out from other traditional job seekers. Check "Willing to Try" for any activity you would consider doing. Then, on a separate sheet, write down some actions you must take to get the ball rolling.

Activity	Willing to Try (yes/no)	Actions to Take
Apply for a job in which I am not interested so that I can practice interviewing.		
Join a professional association. Make connections with people in my field.		
Go to a local college placement office whether or not I attended that college.		
Call up someone famous in my field and ask about trends and new opportunities.		
Buy a product or use a service; then write a letter to the company saying how it can be improved and what I could do to help.		
Volunteer to work for a local civic group in which I can make contacts with new people.		
Find someone who is giving a lecture or paper in my field. Tell that person in advance that I am looking forward to the lecture. Follow up after attending the lecture.		
Contact a temporary agency in my field. Consider an assignment that could gain me good exposure.		
Join a computer bulletin board and make contacts with others in my field.		
Offer my services as a consultant or a freelance worker.		
Start my own business.		
Go to an office building and stop in a number of offices in my field of interest. Get brochures and names of contact people. Then return and ask for an interview.		
Put together a presentation of my work.		
Other innovative ideas:		

$\boxed{2.7}$ Pick Up the Pace

SITUATION

When the mind gets tired, the body lies down. Interpreting your job search as failed, or flawed, or weak, or unproductive will lower your energy level and reduce your pace from a sprint to a crawl. When you recognize rejections as signposts along the way, they will not slow you down.

JOB SEARCH PRINCIPLE TO FOLLOW

Action works.

Wondering what to do is not sufficient. Adding up the reasons to change direction is not the same as taking a step in any direction. It is necessary to bring ideas into practical reality. Take action even though some actions don't yield the results you'd like. Don't get stuck on the notion that everything must work out the way you think it should. The best job search looks something like this:

No, No, No, No, No, No, No, No, No, No, *Yes!!*

Go for the yeses by being willing to encounter more nos, and don't let internal considerations and concerns slow you down. As you start taking daily actions, you'll find yourself more willing to take risks and take the next step after any failure. People who end up in jobs in the dark corners of the workplace are those who sit and wait for the next job to fall into their laps.

STRATEGIC ACTIONS

☞ Along with actions related to your job search, be sure you're taking two or three hours a day off from your job search to engage in exercise, relaxation, and study.

☞ Ask other people in your family circle to keep reminding you that the temporary frustration is just bringing you closer to what will work. Avoid complaining.

☞ Make a copy of the Wall of Nos on page 51. Keep this sheet posted in an area set aside for your job search work. Each time you experience any rejection or failure associated with your job search, cross off another *no* on the sheet. Set a goal to cross off at least ten each week.

The Wall of Nos

No No No No No No No No No No
No No No No No No No No No No
No No No No No No No No No No
No No No No No No No No No No
No No No No No No No No No No
No No No No No No No No No No
No No No No No No No No No No
No No No No No No No No No No
No No No No No No No No No No
No No No No No No No No No No

YES!

2.8 CHANGE DOWNTURNS TO UPTURNS

SITUATION

When economic times are even a little bit tough, the media present disaster scenarios. As a job seeker you'll encounter a lot of reinforcement of the idea that the economy and scarcity of opportunity are making it difficult for you. Don't buy into such self-fulfilling prophecies. Recognize that all you need is one job, and it doesn't matter what the economy is. There's always room for one more productively employed individual—you.

JOB SEARCH PRINCIPLE TO FOLLOW

Don't believe in recessions.

Financial prophets, oracles, and economic statisticians spend most of their time telling you whether the market is going up or down, boom or bust. Every movement is interpreted as part of an ominous next stage: Either we're moving into extreme inflation or deep recession. Recessions come about because people fear the unknown. If people are told that the economy is suffering, they will act accordingly even though the evidence around them indicates otherwise—thus the recession becomes self-fulfilling.

Don't let such ideas affect your own direction. The unemployment rate has nothing to do with you. If you don't have a job, the unemployment rate is 100%. If you do have a job the unemployment rate is zero.

Always be prepared to take the next step to increase your value as a potential employee. Be focused and increase your activity when it feels as though you're slowing down. Many games are won in the last ten minutes of play, but they require sustained action for the entire contest.

STRATEGIC ACTIONS

☞ If you are really concerned about economic difficulties, research which industries are experiencing upward mobility and movement. Concentrate your job search on those.

☞ Even with declining markets and industries, certain aspects of most companies are growing. If you know which industry or field you want to be in, find out which areas within that field are expanding, what new needs are emerging.

☞ In difficult economic times, stress your ability to exercise cost containment measures, to increase effectiveness, to bring in sales, and so on. Tailor your approach to turn around negative or fearful thinking.

☞ When you are clear about your job target, write down four or five ideas you could contribute to help that organization function more effectively and be able to do more with less.

☞ If you're speaking with people in an organization that has been through difficult times, remember that those people are probably a little demoralized and resigned to their difficulties. In your presentation and interview, develop an upbeat approach—not threatening, but inspiring. Talk about the future, not the past; the opportunities, not the needs. Don't be too "pie in the sky," but do carry your positive energy forward into the interview and beyond.

2.9 IT'S NOT IN THE HELP-WANTED ADS

SITUATION

Of course your job search will lead you to the help-wanted advertising. This is a seductive lure on which many people focus their entire job search. Don't be seduced. Don't ignore the want-ads, but don't rely too much on them either.

JOB SEARCH PRINCIPLE TO FOLLOW

Don't depend on the want-ads.

You may not find the job you're looking for in the help-wanted columns or in the listings on placement bulletin boards or in employment agencies. If you do, there may be a lot of competition.

When you look at a job description in an ad, don't believe that you're seeing the complete picture. The ad may list several key duties but omit what really happens on the job. The people who write the advertisements rarely know what really goes on moment to moment in a job. Job requirements change rapidly, so you may be reading a job description that was current last year but has since been revised.

If you don't have a college degree, it doesn't mean you can't have a high-quality job. If you didn't choose the right major, it doesn't mean you can't learn a skill at least as well as others that have been schooled in it. Don't let artificial boundaries of certification and educational requirements stand in your way.

STRATEGIC ACTIONS

☞ Use the yellow pages to identify companies in particular job categories. Get in touch with these companies and try to find out where they're going, whom they have hired, and whom they might hire in the future. Be active in determining how you could help them solve their problems and fill their needs.

☞ If a company advertises a particular opening, you may assume that other organizations in the same field are looking to hire people with similar qualifications. Go to companies that are not advertising now. If one company is building a day care center, for example, you'll probably find others of similar size and location doing or planning to do the same thing.

☞ Go to the archives of your local library and get copies of a newspaper's help-wanted sections from a year or more ago. Look for advertisements for any position that appeals to you. Make a note of the position, the employer, and the employer's address and phone. Use this contact to explore the possible existence of jobs that might be opening up again. Talk with the person who filled the job last time around.

2.10 LISTEN TO YOURSELF

SITUATION

You may think, "If only I were more like X" or "If only I had the energy of Y." Or you may find yourself making comparisons to some other idealized role model. It is a mistake to try to be like somebody else and blame yourself that you are not. Identify those qualities that are best in yourself and develop them.

JOB SEARCH PRINCIPLE TO FOLLOW

Pay attention to your psychology.

Paying attention to your psychology doesn't mean indulging it. Get in touch with your internal barriers. Perhaps you are shy or timid or feel more conservative than innovative. Notice that many of these barriers are simply assumptions that you've made about yourself that don't necessarily have to control your behavior. Give up negative thought if you can, and try to maintain behaviors consistent with a powerful and responsible character.

Much of the way we operate comes from the way we have perceived ourselves or what we've heard said about ourselves. Step away from these old ideas. These inhibiting traits get lost as you move forward assuming the best about yourself. Even if you've had a bad record or been arrested or fired, don't let such a circumstance destroy the outward expression and proactive behavior you need. Admit your mistakes, learn from them, and move on.

STRATEGIC ACTIONS

☞ What are some of the characteristics you use to describe yourself or that others have used to describe you? Are they real or are they imagined? You may label yourself in a way that controls your thinking. Peel away the labels and you will probably find something far better than the self-diminishing characteristics you've applied to yourself. Don't explain yourself or apologize for what you consider to be a shortcoming. Accentuate the positive.

✍ Exercise 24: PERSONALITY PROFILE

In the following list of words, check every word that you feel describes you. Be honest.

___ Aggressive	___ Amiable	___ Brash	___ Intelligent
___ Cautious	___ Creative	___ Dignified	___ Articulate
___ Cynical	___ Competitive	___ Vigorous	
___ Deliberate	___ Devious	___ Flippant	
___ Hurried	___ Energetic	___ Grave	
___ Imperfect	___ Forceful	___ Hard	
___ Impulsive	___ Careful	___ Knowledgeable	
___ Incisive	___ Calculating	___ Limited	
___ Lazy	___ Punctual	___ Motivated	
___ Moody	___ Stable	___ Natural	
___ Merry	___ Modest	___ Organized	
___ Nervous	___ Mature	___ Polite	
___ Literate	___ Humorous	___ Resolute	
___ Stern	___ Poised	___ Stylish	
___ Shrewd	___ Resourceful	___ Remarkable	
___ Shy	___ Honest	___ Versatile	

Add your own:

_____   _____   _____

_____   _____   _____

_____   _____   _____

Of the qualities you checked, which five describe you best?

1. _____

2. _____

3. _____

4. _____

5. _____

Of the qualities you checked, which could be possible barriers to a successful job search?

1. _____

2. _____

3. _____

4. _____

5. _____

Take each item that you just listed and go to Exercise 14 in Chapter 1. Think about the personal assumptions, beliefs, and opinions that keep you boxed in. What is a better view of the situation? Explore different actions that you can take to break down the barriers to your success.

References

How to Find the Perfect Job Tom Jackson (Piatkus)

The Seven Habits of Highly Effective People Stephen Covey (Simon and Schuster)

Handbook for the Positive Revolution Edward de Bono (Penguin)

How to Develop a Positive Attitude Elwood N Chapman (Kogan Page)

Discovering the Hidden Job Market

M ost of us have little idea of how much opportunity lies just beneath the surface of the help-wanted ads. Times of momentous change, especially times of economic instability, make people nervous. They are constantly reminded that "there are no jobs out there" or "good jobs are hard to find."

The very concept of job scarcity bears deeper challenge and investigation, especially as it exacerbates the job seeker's worries and concerns. Even when the unemployment rate is high—say, 10–12%—remember that the *employment* rate is 88–90%. And since some employment is inevitable, the odds are better than ten to one in favor of having a job.

What job? you ask. Most of the jobs available on any given day are not advertised in the help-wanted ads. The hidden job market is the large pool of unadvertised jobs and opportunities that haven't surfaced yet or may never surface in the ads. Job opportunities within the hidden job market arise from organizations in the process of change, as new products are invented and new contracts awarded. Job opportunities exist wherever there are problems or challenges. New opportunities are created with every beat of the economy.

Career entrepreneurism is that process of self-discovery and job creation in which you are the "product" and potential employers are the "buyers."

You penetrate the hidden job market through research and networking. Look beyond the obvious—get on the phone and ask people whom they know who knows somebody who knows someone else. Look beyond your own geography to the world at large and consider consulting, freelancing, and globe-trotting within your job scope.

When you take the view that opportunity abounds, you take off the blinders that prevent you from seeing beyond one job title, profession, or location. You empower yourself to move into the future toward fresh opportunities, to uncover a multitude of job prospects that you might otherwise have passed by.

Key Job Search Principles

3.1 Eighty percent of the available jobs on any given day are not advertised.

3.2 New jobs are created with every beat of the economy.

3.3 Job market research is the key to abundant opportunity.

3.4 Create and use your own referral network.

3.5 Jobs are everywhere.

3.6 People will tell you what you need to know.

3.7 Select, don't settle.

3.8 Pick up the phone.

3.9 Think small.

3.10 Be an entrepreneur or consultant.

3.1 DON'T LIMIT YOURSELF TO ADVERTISED JOBS

SITUATION

You have been looking through the classifieds in the local newspaper for months now. Day after day, week after week, month after month, the same old ads seem to recur.

You ask your friends how they got their jobs and discover that few of them found their current jobs through newspaper ads.

So why are you depending on the help-wanted ads now?

JOB SEARCH PRINCIPLE TO FOLLOW

Eighty percent of the available jobs on any given day are not advertised.

Most job opportunities lie below the visible surface of job postings, help-wanted advertising, and employment-agency or search-firm listings. Jobs are opportunities to solve problems and to address changes in the needs and wants of society. Most of these problems and change opportunities occur long before they are formulated into a particular job description.

Given a tight job market and a surplus of candidates, companies often shun public advertising of vacant positions in order to avoid a deluge of CVs. Instead, the openings might be filled through word of mouth or farmed out to one or two specialized placement agencies.

Jobs that were advertised two or three weeks ago, but do not appear in the current classified section, may still be open or may reflect other growth opportunities within the organization.

STRATEGIC ACTIONS

☞ Think of someone whose retirement is a few months away. His employers might be starting to think about a replacement. They're not ready to run an ad, but they're starting to ask around.

☞ Read the newspapers, business magazines, or trade journals to find companies that have been awarded new contracts. This will start an organization thinking about its needs for new people.

☞ New technologies or market challenges pose new problems. A person able to help provide solutions can often step in and create a job for herself.

✍ Exercise 25: THE HIDDEN JOB MARKET

Get a copy of your local newspaper and discard the classified employment section. Screen the rest of the paper and read the articles pertaining to local developments: A store is expanding, a company has received a new contract, the city is building a new community swimming pool, an executive is retiring, a business owner discusses the growing need for safety. As you read, ask yourself, "What potential jobs could be created as a result of these developments?" List your answers below (include any job, not just those you might consider for yourself).

Reported development: _____

    Potential jobs: _____

_____

_____

Reported development: _____

    Potential jobs: _____

_____

_____

Reported development: _____ _____

  Potential jobs: _____

_____

_____

Reported development: _____

  Potential jobs: _____

_____

_____

3.2 CREATE A JOB

SITUATION

Imagine something like this: Your company keeps a close eye on its competition. A co-worker passes on a rumor that a competing firm is going to face serious problems with a new set of government regulations that will take effect next year. You are very familiar with these regulations and know that your current company will have no problems meeting their requirements. You have a good insight as to how the business can adapt to the changes.

You have been thinking about changing jobs. You have risen as far as you can in your organization and you know that your supervisor will not leave his position for at least a decade.

This is the perfect opportunity to put together a proposal to convince the competing company that it needs to create a new position to keep it informed of proposed regulations and help it adapt to new laws. You are the obvious choice because you can easily create value for the company.

Think of an equivalent example in your own field.

JOB SEARCH PRINCIPLE TO FOLLOW

New jobs are created with every beat of the economy.

By addressing the need of employers to satisfy their customers rather than simply responding to their job postings, you are able to create new employment opportunities for yourself and for the company. A job is an opportunity to solve a problem, and there's no shortage of problems. There is, however, a shortage of people who know how to connect their skills and abilities with existing or arising opportunities.

STRATEGIC ACTIONS

✍ Exercise 26: PROBLEMS INTO OPPORTUNITIES

Go back to Exercise 8 and review the problems you identified as ones you can solve. Take a careful look at how you can turn those problems into opportunities.

What organizations experience these problems?
How can you contribute to helping them solve those problems?
To whom should you talk in the organization?
What is the best strategy for approaching this person?
What can you offer?
What do you want in return?

Organization:_____

Problem to solve:_____

How you can help:_____

_____

Whom to contact:_____

Strategy for approaching this person:_____

What you can offer:_____

_____

What you want in return:_____

_____

Organization:_____

Problem to solve:_____

How you can help:_____

_____

Whom to contact:_____

Strategy for approaching this person:_____

What you can offer:_____

_____

What you want in return:_____

_____

33 RESEARCH, RESEARCH, RESEARCH

SITUATION

You've decided to focus your efforts toward a specific job target. You have a clear idea of your target, and you know what skills and capabilities you can offer a potential employer. Now you need to take the next step: finding the names of all the employers in your region that hire people in your target area or have problems that someone like you can help solve.

Offhand, you can name a few well-known employers in your community that hire people like you. But who else could utilize your services?

JOB SEARCH PRINCIPLE TO FOLLOW

Job market research is the key to abundant opportunity.

In this country we are blessed with a powerful, extensive information and data retrieval system. From your home computer or local library, you can gain access to names of all kinds of potential employers in just a few hours of focused research. Major source books include directories of directories, directories of publications, and directories of associations.

STRATEGIC ACTIONS

☞ Find sources of information on potential employers:

- At your local library, ask the reference librarian to help you find information (printed and from computer data bases) about employers in your target field.
- If you are in college or near one, ask a career counselor to help you research potential employers.
- Visit your local chamber of commerce.
- In the yellow pages of your phone directory you can locate listings for companies that provide products or services related to your job target area.

☞ Read back issues of newspapers.

- Look for job listings in your target area in last year's paper.
- Call each employer and ask to speak to the person who was hired for the advertised position, or to that person's manager.

- Find out how that person becomes aware of job openings in his or her own or other organizations.

☞ Contact the headquarters of the professional associations that work with people in your job target area.

  - Ask them to direct you to their reference libraries.
  - Get copies of trade journals and other publications that contain information about the state of the industry, its leadership, new products and services, and recognized authorities in the field.
  - Contact the authors of the articles or editors of the publications.

☞ Review corporate annual reports, available from most brokerage firms at no charge.

  - Look for trends, problems, and the company's overall position in the industry.
  - Get names of key officers and executives.
  - Find out about competitors.

☞ Keep up with your general reading.

  - Read newspapers and newsmagazines. Clip articles that pertain to your target area to stay in touch with new developments, changes, and trends.
  - Keep abreast of new books and publications. Learn the names of the authors, experts, and other successful people in your field. Contact them.

✍ Exercise 27: SOURCING

Locate a minimum of five prime sources of information about potential jobs in your field. Name the sources related to each of your job targets.

Job target:_____

  Prime sources: A._____

               B._____

               C._____

               D._____

               E._____

Job target:_____ ____ _____

    Prime sources: A._____

                 B._____

                 C._____

                 D._____

                 E._____

Job target:_____

    Prime sources: A._____

                 B._____

                 C._____

                 D._____

                 E._____

Now use these sources to uncover actual employer names and addresses.

3.4   YOU ARE NOT ALONE

SITUATION

You feel alone. You keep the fact that you are looking for a job a secret, feeling embarrassed about being unemployed. There must be something wrong with you if you are not productively employed. You've done a lot to help others in the past, but now that it's your turn to receive help from others, you feel uncomfortable asking for assistance.

JOB SEARCH PRINCIPLE TO FOLLOW

Create and use your own referral network.

You must know somebody who knows somebody who knows somebody else . . . and, to paraphrase an old adage, you're perhaps as few as six steps away from almost anyone of interest in the world.

    The organized and aggressive use of personal referral networks is the hallmark of a good job searcher. Networks can be used to acquire contacts, feedback, introductions, coaching, and counseling. Consider networks as sources of information that may lead you to jobs—not as sources of jobs themselves.

STRATEGIC ACTIONS

✍ Exercise 28: NETWORKING

Start with the names of your friends and move to professional associates, teachers, and ex-employers. Include people you know in associations or professional groups who might know others, and build a list of at least one hundred potential contacts who might be willing to accept a phone call and spend three or four minutes telling you what they know.

Your personal support network
  Includes: family, relatives, friends, neighbors, clergy, etc. See page 46.
  Can provide: moral support, personal feedback, financial assistance, baby-sitting, help with typing CVs or cover letters, etc.

Dates Contacted

Name: _____ Phone: _____
Ways to help: _____
_____

Name: _____ Phone: _____
Ways to help: _____
_____

Name: _____ Phone: _____
Ways to help: _____
_____

Name: _____ Phone: _____
Ways to help: _____
_____

Add more on your own.

Your professional network
  Includes: former co-workers and supervisors, teachers/professors, authors, consultants

Can provide: contacts in your field, introductions and referrals, information on trends, career advice

Dates Contacted

Name: _____ Phone: _____ Ways to help: _____ _____			

Name: _____ Phone: _____ Ways to help: _____ _____			

Name: _____ Phone: _____ Ways to help: _____ _____			

Name: _____ Phone: _____ Ways to help: _____ _____			

Add more on your own.

Your career support network

Includes: executive recruiters, college placement officers, career counselors
Can provide: information, referrals, counseling

Dates Contacted

Name: _____ Phone: _____ Ways to help: _____ _____			

Name: _____ Phone: _____ Ways to help: _____ _____			

Name: _____	Phone: _____				
Ways to help: _____					
_____					

Name: _____	Phone: _____				
Ways to help: _____					
_____					

Add more on your own

[3.5] NO SCARCITY

SITUATION

Your hometown was built around a handful of major employers. In the past, just about everyone worked for one of those companies, but during the last decade many of them have been taken over by a larger conglomerate, operations have moved elsewhere, or the businesses have been downsized. Opportunity for employment in these companies looks bleak at best. Even civil service jobs are being cut back. Should you give up and look for work somewhere else? Or is there hope of finding a job close to home?

JOB SEARCH PRINCIPLE TO FOLLOW

Jobs are everywhere.

You make a mistake when you identify job openings primarily with corporate facilities and major towns and cities. Organizations of all types have smaller outposts and subsidiaries, and even contract work is available virtually everywhere.

Also, an increasing number of businesses are honoring the needs of people who want to work at home on a part-time or freelance basis. The "corporate office at home" is gaining in popularity as employers realize that valuable time is lost in commuting, and that maintaining facilities and administration at a corporate headquarters for full-time employees is expensive.

✍ **Exercise 29: TWENTY EMPLOYER PROSPECTS**

Using the research sources from Exercise 27, create a list of a minimum of twenty potential employers located within thirty miles of your home for each job target. (Make copies of the form for additional targets.)

Include the employer's name, address, phone number, and the key person in charge of hiring for your field.

Job target:_____

1. Employer:_____ Phone:_____

   Location:_____ Key contact:_____

2. Employer:_____ Phone:_____

   Location:_____ Key contact:_____

3. Employer:_____ Phone:_____

   Location:_____ Key contact:_____

4. Employer:_____ Phone:_____

   Location:_____ Key contact:_____

5. Employer:_____ Phone:_____

   Location:_____ Key contact:_____

6. Employer:_____ Phone:_____

   Location:_____ Key contact:_____

7. Employer:_____ Phone:_____

   Location:_____ Key contact:_____

8. Employer:_____ Phone:_____

   Location:_____ Key contact:_____

9. Employer:_____ Phone:_____

   Location:_____ Key contact:_____

10. Employer:_____ Phone:_____

    Location:_____ Key contact:_____

11. Employer:_____ Phone:_____

    Location:_____ Key contact:_____

12. Employer:_____ Phone:_____

    Location:_____ Key contact:_____

13. Employer:_____ Phone:_____

    Location:_____ Key contact:_____

14. Employer:＿＿＿＿＿＿＿＿＿＿＿ Phone:＿＿＿＿＿＿＿＿＿＿＿
    Location:＿＿＿＿＿＿＿＿＿＿＿ Key contact:＿＿＿＿＿＿＿＿＿

15. Employer:＿＿＿＿＿＿＿＿＿＿＿ Phone:＿＿＿＿＿＿＿＿＿＿＿
    Location:＿＿＿＿＿＿＿＿＿＿＿ Key contact:＿＿＿＿＿＿＿＿＿

16. Employer:＿＿＿＿＿＿＿＿＿＿＿ Phone:＿＿＿＿＿＿＿＿＿＿＿
    Location:＿＿＿＿＿＿＿＿＿＿＿ Key contact:＿＿＿＿＿＿＿＿＿

17. Employer:＿＿＿＿＿＿＿＿＿＿＿ Phone:＿＿＿＿＿＿＿＿＿＿＿
    Location:＿＿＿＿＿＿＿＿＿＿＿ Key contact:＿＿＿＿＿＿＿＿＿

18. Employer:＿＿＿＿＿＿＿＿＿＿＿ Phone:＿＿＿＿＿＿＿＿＿＿＿
    Location:＿＿＿＿＿＿＿＿＿＿＿ Key contact:＿＿＿＿＿＿＿＿＿

19. Employer:＿＿＿＿＿＿＿＿＿＿＿ Phone:＿＿＿＿＿＿＿＿＿＿＿
    Location:＿＿＿＿＿＿＿＿＿＿＿ Key contact:＿＿＿＿＿＿＿＿＿

20. Employer:＿＿＿＿＿＿＿＿＿＿＿ Phone:＿＿＿＿＿＿＿＿＿＿＿
    Location:＿＿＿＿＿＿＿＿＿＿＿ Key contact:＿＿＿＿＿＿＿＿＿

3.6 INTERVIEW FOR INFORMATION AND RELATIONSHIPS

SITUATION

You're reasonably clear about the career change you want to make. You've focused on two or three new fields in which you know you can make a contribution and that should give you more satisfaction. The problem is that you haven't had much experience in these areas. Even though you are confident of your capabilities, you're not rich in contacts and day-to-day information. You read the trade journals and pay attention to every piece of information that you come across, but you still feel you don't measure up. You need to strengthen your ability to discuss the field and feel comfortable in a conversation or interview.

JOB SEARCH PRINCIPLE TO FOLLOW

People will tell you what you need to know.

Once you've chosen a career path that fits your basic skills, interests, and qualities, you need to expand your day-to-day conversational ability in this field. It is important to talk with people in the field who can acquaint you with the current state of the industry or profession.

The idea of **information interviews** is to meet with ten or so people working in your field, solely for the purpose of finding out what's happening, to sharpen your language skills, and to build your base of information. These are not employment interviews, and you need to be careful about not crossing the line between doing research and asking for a job.

STRATEGIC ACTIONS

☞ Strategies for the information interview:

- Have your questions written down, and keep the meeting professional, to the point, and on time. If you had requested twenty minutes, be sure to honor that, and as the clock approaches the twenty-minute mark, get ready to wrap it up.

- Let your information build. After each interview record what you've learned and what else you need to learn in the next interview.

- Always remember that you are primarily interested in obtaining information about potential employers.

- Have your questions prepared before calling or meeting with one of your resources. Be able to demonstrate that you are sincerely interested in obtaining information and leads.

- Find out about the kinds of problems in the industry, the latest developments in products and services, and the qualifications and qualities employers are looking for in employees.

- Ask for names of other people in your field to see.

- Send out a well-prepared thank-you letter after each meeting with a personal contact.

- Keep a record of your contacts.

- Leave two or three copies of your CV with your contacts to forward to anyone they think might be interested in exploring opportunities with you.

- *Do not be tempted to switch the discussion from information gathering to the possibility of employment with that employer.* If the contact asks, obviously you can follow her lead. However, if you restrict the interview to information gathering, you will gain the respect of the contact, who will let you know if there are openings.

✍ **Exercise 30: INFORMATION INTERVIEWS**

Identify at least three topics or areas in which having better inside information would improve your standing in the job market and help you in making a more informed career choice. Use the form below to write down your topic and a key person whom you can contact for an information interview. Set up a time for the interview. Afterward record any actions you can take to follow up on what you learned.

Information interview topic:_____

Contact:_____   Company:_____

Meeting date:_____   Phone: _____

Follow-up actions:_____

_____

_____

Information interview topic:_____

Contact:_____   Company:_____

Meeting date:_____   Phone:_____

Follow-up actions:_____ _____

_____ _ _____

_____

Information interview topic:_____

Contact:_____   Company:_____

Meeting date:_____   Phone:_____

Follow-up actions:_____

_____

_____

3.7 GOING FOR THE GOLD—SELECTING THE BEST

SITUATION

Success! You've received one firm offer, and there are one or two possibilities that look as though they'll develop into offers. Your life has moved from one of worry and concern, focused on scarcity, to one of abundance. You breathe a great big sigh of relief. Then you examine the offer again, and something tells you that maybe you ought to stall your response a little and give it a bit more thought. Remember, your last job turned out to be not exactly what you wanted. Take the time to be selective.

Job Search Principle to Follow

Select, don't settle.

The effect of self-marketing strategies, as described in this book and others, should lead you to a variety of opportunities. Don't make the mistake of jumping on the first offer that comes along simply to avoid the effort of searching further.

A true career master learns how to attract several offers and evaluate their ability to fulfill his range of personal and career requirements. Keep in mind the criteria you're looking for in your next employer, and then measure any job opportunity against these criteria. If the criteria are not met, continue to search—unless you're desperately out of funds or your psyche can't stand the strain.

Strategic Actions

☞ If you've received only one offer, you may feel pressed to make a decision from fear that this is the only option available to you. Do what you can to stall the first offer until you see what others might be pulled together. Examine closely your motivations for wanting to accept the first offer. Pose the question: "Is this where I want to be for the next five years of my life?"

☞ It is okay—actually recommended—to let the employer know that you need a little time to consider her offer. The "thinking" time may vary from situation to situation. In some cases you might ask for a week or ten days; in others you may need to move more quickly.

☞ You will want to review a variety of factors when deciding whether or not to accept an offer. Consider the following criteria, and modify this list to include other factors important to you that we haven't suggested:

Growth potential: Will you be able to grow with the job or field? Is the industry expanding? Has the organization shown a steady rate of profit? Within the job itself, is there good reason to expect that you will develop new skills and responsibilities that will enable you to rise to your highest level of competence?

Compensation: Will you earn what you are worth? How well do others in the company or industry get paid in comparable jobs? Do the benefits (vacation, health insurance, profit sharing, expense accounts, pensions, etc.) add value to the compensation package?

Lifestyle: How does the job measure up to your needs for work satisfaction? Can you dress as you want? Can you define your work hours to fit in with your obligations at home? Will you have your own work space? Are there social opportunities?

Performance: Are you expected to develop along with the job, or is routine performance expected? Is there on-the-job training to improve your skills? How does your job fit into the overall structure of the organization? Who will supervise you? How much authority or autonomy will you have? Is the work laid out for you, or is there room for innovation? What will challenge you to improve your performance?

Other criteria: Are there any other aspects of a job that are important to you that haven't been mentioned (learning, travel, etc.)? Keep these in mind. Also think about any factors that would automatically disqualify a job in your mind.

☞ If you do not yet have enough information to rate employers, return to your network or contact someone in the field. People who can help furnish you with information are:

- Other employers
- Employees working in the field
- Authors and editors of publications in the field
- Trade associations
- College placement counselors

3.8 TELEMARKETING YOURSELF

SITUATION

Many job seekers end up running a mail-order campaign. You send out a barrage of CVs and cover letters in response to the help-wanteds and employment-agency listings. In return you receive form letters, applications, and rejections. Instinctively, you tend to avoid one-on-one contact with people whom you don't know. You don't like to be in the position of asking strangers for help. You certainly don't want to be turned down. And yet, in order to create the momentum you need, you must make personal contact.

Job Search Principle to Follow

Pick up the phone.

All the theories, strategies, and tactics in the world will not connect you to potential employers until you take sustained action. The telephone is your best ally in uncovering potential jobs. Use it regularly and in an organized fashion. When you have a large number of possible contacts, you don't have so much at stake when you're turned down or you can't get through on any given call.

The best job searches are inevitably comprised of a series of nos followed by yeses. The faster you get through the nos, the faster you'll get to the yeses. (See Section 2.7.) Phone fright is natural at first. Once you've had some practice you'll swing into action with vigor, following a daily routine to cut a clear path to the results you desire.

Strategic Actions

☞   Follow these steps in preparing for your telephone contacts.

- Make a list of the people you want to contact each day. Don't work off of a long master list. The task of contacting everyone on such a list can be intimidating; instead, make a list of five individuals whom you intend to call within a given time.

- Reread everything in your files about the organization. Make some notes of key words and phrases that you feel will help you communicate. You don't want to read your presentation, but notes will help you remember what to say.

- Practice what to say in advance.

- Be sure you know the name and title of the person you wish to reach.

- Remember that your purpose for calling is to get the employer to agree to meet you. "The reason I'm calling is to see if we can set up a short meeting. I'd like to show you some examples of my work and find out some more about what you are doing. Can we meet tomorrow afternoon?" Do not try to interview the employer or sell yourself over the phone.

- Pick up the phone and go! Make all the calls you can in one sitting. Stop for no more than five minutes between each call to review what happened in the previous call and to plan your strategy for the next one.

✍ Exercise 31: CONTACT LOG

Prepare a 3 × 5 inch index card or computer record for each contact you want
to make before your phone call. Use the following format or one similar.

Telephone contact log

Side A

Employer:_____ Phone:_____

    Address:_____

    Contact:_____

    Secretary's name:_____

    Objective:_____

    Key points to make:_____

    _____

    _____

    _____

Side B

    Results:_____

    _____

    _____

    _____

    Follow-up actions to take (show date):_____

    _____

    _____

    _____

    _____

[3.9] SMALL IS BEAUTIFUL

SITUATION

You've researched and contacted all the major employers in your community, and you've learned that budgets are tight. Your part of the state has the lowest unemployment rate, but you constantly hear from your contacts that no one is even considering hiring at this time. Where are all the jobs?

While waiting for a dental appointment, you pick up a magazine called *Today's Business*, targeted at small businesses in your community. You have not heard of most of the small businesses featured in the magazine; they are not listed in the directories and other sources you consulted in the library.

Through research you learn that most of these businesses are start-up companies employing five to fifty individuals. Some are having problems keeping up with their rate of growth. There is no fat in their budgets, so they cannot afford to hire people who will not work at top performance and produce results. The starting pay may not be competitive with the larger companies, but the opportunity for growing with the business and sharing in its success is great.

JOB SEARCH PRINCIPLE TO FOLLOW

Think small.

Big opportunities can come in small packages. There are thousands of small organizations in every line of work. Quite frequently they are invisible to the man on the street or the reader of business publications. They usually don't make the news, and they're not on anybody's list of the biggest and most productive organizations. However, they can be the most exciting places at which to work. Small firms are formed around new technologies, new services, and new markets. They are often made up of people with fresh resources, energy, and a venturesome spirit.

STRATEGIC ACTIONS

☞ Spend a couple of hours with your local business telephone directory. Peruse the varieties of headings and advertisements. Brainstorm as you read the names of these businesses, many of which are small establishments. Continue reading under "Business Services" and "Consultants" and note small firms among them. Circle a few that you want to call. Talk to their owners, ask how they got started and what kinds of people they look to hire. Ask if you may visit.

☞ If you know the larger companies in your job search area, you may be able to consult them for the names of the smaller organizations that provide training, consulting, and other services to them. Use your information interviewing techniques to uncover leads to smaller, less visible firms.

3.10 BE YOUR OWN BOSS

SITUATIONS

- All your life you have dreamed of owning your own business, but never believed that you could do it. That's something that other people do, people with lots of money to get started. Still, you have the right ideas and know what product or service you want to sell. Why not look into the details of going into business for yourself? What's stopping you from at least speaking to others who have followed that path?

- You've just had your first child and want to devote the next few years to her. You want to stay current with your field, and can work part-time for a few hours each week. You have skills that businesses need, and can offer yourself as a consultant.

JOB SEARCH PRINCIPLE TO FOLLOW

Be an entrepreneur or consultant.

Career entrepreneurism is the art of seeing yourself as a valuable product. You are continually looking for situations in which you can be an asset to an organization. Career entrepreneurism requires that you maintain your skills and capabilities and present them in a way so they are clearly seen as valuable. Career entrepreneurism requires an investment in yourself through education, coaching, and counseling. It requires preparation of CVs and a well-organized ongoing career development plan.

Akin to career entrepreneurism is running a small business or consulting service. This should always be considered if you are in a field of high-level expertise or in a marketplace that has a high demand for your particular skills. Setting up a small business is an exciting way to manifest the combination of your skills and interests. It requires a careful and astute marketing plan, a budget, and the persistence to go through many months of preliminaries and development.

Strategic Actions

☞ There are usually two or three publications, monthly or quarterly, of interest to entrepreneurs. These publications can be found in an index to periodicals. Look through them for references and ideas.

☞ If you have a specific idea of the business you want to set up, you can go to another location and find somebody in a similar business who, since you will not be a competitor, might give you some good ideas and insights. You could consider working out a consulting arrangement by which you offer him a fee for assisting you.

☞ It is useful to team up with someone who already has experience in the consulting or service fields. Use her as a mentor or partner and find a way to combine office expenses.

☞ In considering how to charge for your services, the rule of thumb is to take what you might normally earn as a salary, calculate its daily rate, and multiply by three: one third for marketing, one third for the actual services, and one third for the overhead of running your own show.

☞ If you are seriously thinking about going into business, ask yourself these questions to determine your level of interest and commitment:

- What product or service do I want to offer?
- Who is the customer for this product or service?
- What value does this product or service provide the customer?
- Does the product or service produce more value for the customer than it costs?
- Can I produce the product or service for significantly less than its selling price?
- How am I going to communicate this value to the customer?
- Are my methods of communication going to generate sales?
- How am I going to set up a predetermined business plan?
- How am I going to manage my business and measure its success against this plan?
- What amount of capital do I need to get my business going?
- How am I going to ensure that I have enough capital to get through a worst-case scenario?

References

Guerrilla Tactics in the new Job Market Tom Jackson (Bantam)

What Color Is Your Parachute? Richard N. Bolles (Ten Speed Press)

Networks Tim Heald (Coronet)

Networking and Mentoring—A Woman's Guide Dr Lily Segerman Peck (Piatkus)

Power CVs

A power CV is a CV that opens doors for you. The power CV is not an application, personnel file or biography. It is a concise advertisement for yourself that communicates your value and creates employers' interest in interviewing you.

In preparing a CV you always want to look toward the future and toward your job targets, to use the information from the past to support your focus on the future. When a CV focuses too much on the past it becomes static and inert, leaving the employer with the task of digging for possibilities. By customizing your CV you can provide succinct, focused marketing communications specific to each employer you want to reach. Your CV is then no longer junk mail, but an offer of value.

There are many varieties and formats of CVs from which to choose. Take the time to create the CV that works for you.

In all your communications, whether in the form of a CV, cover letter, or interview, you want to use language that is direct, concise, and powerful.

Key Job Search Principles

4.1 A CV is not an application

4.2 Communicating value is key.

4.3 A CV should be about the future, not the past.

4.4 Customize your CV for each possibility.

4.5 Choose the format that works best for you in each situation.

4.6 Use power language.

4.7 Make a first-class presentation.

4.1 AN INVITATION TO INTERVIEW

SITUATION

You've accumulated a wealth of experience, information, education, and valuable accomplishments that make up the warp and woof of your career. You may be tempted to create a massive document that could be called "The Story of My Life." Don't. By its nature, a CV is a distillate, a precious concentration of those things that are most interesting to an employer. More information can be provided later if needed.

JOB SEARCH PRINCIPLE TO FOLLOW

A CV is not an application.

CVs are often greatly misunderstood. People treat them as personnel files, job applications, or detailed histories.

In our view, the CV has only one purpose: to get you an interview. Once you have the interview, you can then offer more expanded information as requested. Without the interview, nothing happens.

Like any good advertisement, a CV needs to be short and to the point. It needs to address what the employer (buyer) needs, not only the product's asset.

The CV needs to look good and present a clear selling message. It needs to open doors for future possibilities with employers who interest you.

Strategic Actions

☞ If you are responding to an advertisement or a job description that matches your job target, review the job description and underline those qualifications that are most valuable to the employer. Once you have completed your CV, check it against these underlined points to see if the CV is responsive to what's needed.

☞ Be prepared to have two or three different CVs with different emphases for different job directions or employers.

✍ Exercise 32: IMPRESSIONS

Imagine for a few minutes that you have the perfect CV, one that clearly communicates who you are in a way that will motivate an employer to pick up the phone and invite you in for an interview. In spending just a few seconds scanning your CV, the employer receives a very positive impression of you and knows that you are the right person to interview.

What are the impressions that you want to leave with the employer? Complete the following statement for at least five potential employers.

EXAMPLE

I want the employer to think that I _can increase sales and profits through effective customer service techniques._

The way I can demonstrate this is by _explaining how I increased subscription renewal rates for the school newspaper._

---

1. I want the employer to think that I _____

_____

The way I can demonstrate this is by_____

_____

2. I want the employer to think that I _____

_____

The way I can demonstrate this is by_____

_____

3. I want the employer to think that I _____

_____

The way I can demonstrate this is by_____

_____

4. I want the employer to think that I _____

_____

The way I can demonstrate this is by_____

_____

5. I want the employer to think that I _____

_____

The way I can demonstrate this is by_____

_____

✍ Exercise 33: PERFORMANCE QUALITIES CHECKLIST

Your CV must also communicate (overtly or indirectly) that you have the qualities of an exceptional employee and high performer. Here is a list of performance qualities. Go through this list and check any quality you want to communicate about yourself in your CV. Add any other qualities that you want to communicate about yourself to this list.

_____ Have a good understanding of business
_____ Make valuable suggestions
_____ Concentrate on getting the job done
_____ Put strong emphasis on quality results
_____ Follow procedures accurately
_____ Exhibit leadership ability
_____ Take care of equipment and property
_____ Show loyalty
_____ Take risks
_____ Communicate clearly
_____ Maintain positive energy
_____ Maintain self-discipline
_____ Work effectively under pressure
_____ Concentrate in spite of distractions
_____ Demonstrate versatility

_____ Understand how profits are created
_____ Perform well in emergencies
_____ Show initiative
_____ Analyze complex problems
_____ Plan well and use time effectively
_____ Work effectively on a team
_____ Train people well
_____ Energize and motivate others
_____ Accept changes easily
_____ Adapt to new conditions
_____ Rise to new challenges
_____ Show good workmanship
_____ Accept criticism
_____ Perform physically exhausting work
_____ Challenge old ways of thinking
_____ Manifest high personal standards

_____   _____

_____   _____

_____   _____

List the three most important performance qualities you want to communicate on your CV and an example of the quality in action.

1.   I want my CV to convey the **quality** that I can _____

_____

An example of this is_____

_____

_____

_____

2.   I want my CV to convey the **quality** that I can _____

_____

An example of this is_____

_____

_____

_____

3.   I want my CV to convey the **quality** that I can _____

_____

An example of this is_____

_____

_____

_____

4.2 A VALUE-ADDED CV

SITUATION

You think you have come up with an easy way to write your CV: You will just take your current job description and condense it into a few sentences. Since your job description lists all of your most current responsibilities and duties, you reason that they will make an impressive beginning to your CV.

Think again. Will a prospective employer know how well you did on the job? Anyone can be given responsibilities, but not all produce tangible results. Perhaps simply copying your job description isn't such a good idea after all.

JOB SEARCH PRINCIPLE TO FOLLOW

Communicating value is key.

Your CV, like all your communications to employers, needs to make the point that you can add significant value to their company. Your interaction with employers should address the *employer's* interests as well as your own. Include your accomplishments, not simply your job duties. Speak to opportunities capitalized upon and problems solved, not just past assignments. If possible, quantify and specify the value that you have produced in terms that an employer can understand (bottom-line pounds, contracts, billings, etc.).

STRATEGIC ACTIONS

☞ Your CV must communicate two messages to a potential employer:

(1) You have the capability to do the work that needs to be done.
(2) You can produce tangible results for the employer.

On your CV specify your skills, knowledge, and ability to do the work in your job target area. Your ability to produce future results can be demonstrated by describing results you have produced in the past.

✍ Exercise 34: SIGNIFICANT CAPABILITIES

In the list below check any word that relates to something that you *can do* in your job target area and want to highlight on your CV:

____ Create	____ Write	____ Refer	____ Instruct	____ Diagnose
____ Serve	____ Plan	____ Assist	____ Evaluate	____ Network
____ Reduce	____ Produce	____ Negotiate	____ Conduct	____ Complete
____ Deliver	____ Observe	____ Sell	____ Study	____ Order
____ Improve	____ Design	____ Consult	____ Increase	____ Supply
____ Evaluate	____ Train	____ Invent	____ Calculate	____ Administer
____ Identify	____ Maintain	____ Examine	____ Perform	____ Restore
____ Construct	____ Advise	____ Process	____ Control	____ Lecture
____ Review	____ Dispense	____ Criticize	____ Translate	____ Chart

____ Formulate	____ Prescribe	____ Improve	____ Reward	____ Oversee
____ Test	____ Purchase	____ Represent	____ Protect	____ Program
____ Promote	____ Obtain	____ Install	____ Record	____ Supervise
____ Route	____ Operate	____ Render	____ Counsel	____ Organize
____ Correspond	____ Audit	____ Draw up	____ Strategize	____ Build
____ Coordinate	____ Receive	____ Research	____ Present	____ Devise
____ Implement	____ Expand	____ Detect	____ Log	____ Direct
____ Recommend	____ Institute	____ Prepare	____ Interview	____ Distribute
____ Interpret	____ Select	____ Manage	____ Provide	____ Conserve
____ Eliminate	____ Discover	____ Arrange	____ Develop	____ Determine
____ Disprove	____ Solve	____ Arbitrate	____ Navigate	____ Acquire
____ Assemble	____ Edit	____ Collect	____ Analyze	____ _____
____ Sing	____ Draw	____ Compose	____ _____	____ _____
____ _____	____ _____	____ _____	____ _____	____ _____

Looking at the words that you checked, complete ten to fifteen capability statements that clearly communicate your skills, knowledge, or ability in your job target area.

Regarding my job target, I can _manage product development teams_.

Regarding my job target:

I can _____

I can _____

I can _____

I can _____

I can _____

I can _____

I can _____

I can _____

I can _____

I can _____

I can _____

I can _____

I can _____

I can _____

I can _____

Review these capability statements. Do they communicate that you are able to do the work that needs to be done in your job target field?

✍ Exercise 35: SIGNIFICANT ACCOMPLISHMENTS

Check any word in the list below that relates to something that you *have done* in past jobs or nonwork activities:

____ Created	____ Wrote	____ Referred	____ Instructed	____ Analyzed
____ Programmed	____ Planned	____ Assisted	____ Evaluated	____ Diagnosed
____ Administered	____ Produced	____ Negotiated	____ Conducted	____ Networked
____ Delivered	____ Observed	____ Sold	____ Studied	____ Completed
____ Improved	____ Designed	____ Consulted	____ Increased	____ Ordered
____ Evaluated	____ Trained	____ Invented	____ Calculated	____ Supplied
____ Identified	____ Examined	____ Performed	____ Reduced	____ Constructed
____ Advised	____ Processed	____ Controlled	____ Restored	____ Reviewed
____ Translated	____ Criticized	____ Lectured	____ Prescribed	____ Formulated
____ Interviewed	____ Rewarded	____ Charted	____ Improved	____ Purchased
____ Protected	____ Oversaw	____ Promoted	____ Obtained	____ Installed
____ Recorded	____ Served	____ Routed	____ Operated	____ Rendered
____ Supervised	____ Audited	____ Drew up	____ Counseled	____ Organized
____ Coordinated	____ Received	____ Researched	____ Built	____ Implemented
____ Expanded	____ Detected	____ Presented	____ Devised	____ Instituted
____ Interpreted	____ Logged	____ Directed	____ Prepared	____ Selected
____ Managed	____ Tested	____ Distributed	____ Eliminated	____ Arranged
____ Conserved	____ Provided	____ Disproved	____ Solved	____ Arbitrated
____ Determined	____ Developed	____ Assembled	____ Edited	____ Collected
____ Navigated	____ Acquired	____ Sang	____ Drew	____ Composed

____ _____ ____ _____ ____ _____ ____ _____ ____ _____
____ _____ ____ _____ ____ _____ ____ _____ ____ _____

Reviewing the words that you checked, complete ten to fifteen accomplishment statements that clearly communicate your ability to produce results in your job target area:

EXAMPLE

Regarding my job target, I have <u>counseled people in life-change situations.</u>

Regarding my job target:

I have _____

I have _____

I have _____

I have _____

I have _____

I have _____

I have _____

I have _____

I have _____

I have _____

I have _____

I have _____

I have _____

I have _____

I have _____

Review your accomplishment statements. Do these communicate that you can produce results? Look for ways to revise these statements so they make a stronger impression.

4.3 YOUR CV IS NOT YOUR BIOGRAPHY

SITUATION

You've come a long way: You've graduated from school, served in the military, worked at a number of good jobs, participated in a variety of professional activities, won a few awards, volunteered for a few organizations, raised a family—the list goes on and on. Looking back over your career, you feel proud and confident that the employer will agree on how well you've done. But think about it. Are you dealing in the past, present, or future tense?

Job Search Principle to Follow

A CV should be about the future, not the past.

Customarily, people prepare CVs that inventory and emphasize past activities, past jobs, past education, etc. We recommend you use the CV as a forward-looking document. We suggest that you prepare several CVs, each with a specific job target in mind, and that all information—including past job history and education—be expressed in a way that relates to future targets. Your CV will of course include dates, times, places, job history, etc; however, this information should be focused to demonstrate why you should be hired for a particular *future* situation.

Strategic Actions

✍ • Exercise 36: LINKING PAST TO FUTURE

Fill out the following inventory of work and nonwork experiences. Think about how each of these experiences relates to your current job target. On the right, list specific skills you developed as a result of the experience that relates to your current job target. You may not use all of this information on your CV; however, completing this process will help you speak clearly about your capabilities and experiences in a job interview.

High School Experiences	How Do These Experiences Contribute to Success in Your Future Job Target?
Best subjects:_____	_____
_____	_____
_____	_____
Extracurricular activities:_____	_____
_____	_____
_____	_____
Awards and honors:_____	_____
_____	_____
_____	_____

College

Best subjects:_____	_____
_____	_____
_____	_____

Extracurricular activities:_____ _____

_____ _____

_____ _____

Awards and honors:_____ _____

_____ _____

_____ _____

Other achievements and activities:__ _____

_____ _____

_____ _____

Military Experience and Training
Activities:_____ _____

_____ _____

_____ _____

_____ _____

_____ _____

Awards and honors:_____ _____

_____ _____

_____ _____

Home and Community Work
Activities and accomplishments:____ _____

_____ _____

_____ _____

_____ _____

_____ _____

Hobbies and Special Interests
Hobby or activity:_____ _____

_____ _____

Hobby or activity:_____ _____

_____ _____

Hobby or activity:_____ _____

_____ _____

Employment

Employer and position:_____   _____

_____   _____

Accomplishments on this job:_____   _____

_____   _____

_____   _____

_____   _____

_____   _____

_____   _____

Employer and position:_____   _____

_____   _____

Accomplishments on this job:_____   _____

_____   _____

_____   _____

_____   _____

_____   _____

_____   _____

Employer and position:_____   _____

_____   _____

Accomplishments on this job:_____   _____

_____   _____

_____   _____

_____   _____

_____   _____

_____   _____

Employer and position:_____   _____

_____   _____

Accomplishments on this job:_____   _____

_____   _____

_____   _____

_____   _____

_____   _____

_____   _____

Honors, Awards, Professional Societies, etc.

_____   _____
_____   _____
_____   _____
_____   _____
_____   _____

4.4 THE "ALL-PURPOSE" CV IS OBSOLETE

SITUATION

Imagine that you are an employer staying late at work. You have to read through sixty CVs sitting on your desk, hoping to find someone to take over for your grant writer who left unexpectedly last week.

Here's a CV from a recent college graduate. He majored in English (that's encouraging), but his CV speaks about the jobs he held in school: pizza deliveryman, lifeguard, and library aide. Does he know how to write grant proposals? It's hard to say.

Here's another CV, from a woman who managed a community-based program that helps persons with disabilities live independent lives. Her CV speaks about her ability to work with diverse populations and to coordinate services with other community agencies. She must have had experience writing grant proposals, but her CV doesn't mention it.

You're discouraged. Your announcement clearly stated that you want someone to write grant proposals, but instead you're being given a lot of information that you really don't want. Not one of the applicants tells you about his or her ability or experience in writing grant proposals. You wish you could give all applicants a piece of advice.

JOB SEARCH PRINCIPLE TO FOLLOW

Customize your CV for each possibility.

With the advent of word processing and computerized CV kits, it is now possible to customize your CV efficiently to each employment opportunity—to organize information so that you are speaking to the needs of the employer. Customizing your CV to the needs of a particular employer, field, or location strengthens your communication. Just as in advertising, the game in the job search process is to pinpoint particular buyers. By adding a customized cover letter, you will create a powerful strategic communication that can greatly enhance your ability to get the interviews you want.

STRATEGIC ACTIONS

☞ Set yourself up with a computer or word processor so that as you develop focused paragraphs to use on particular CVs, you can save them for later retrieval and use.

✍ Exercise 37: INFORMATION SELECTION

If you *really* want to capture the attention of a particular employer, you need to take the time to customize your CV so that it speaks directly to his needs.

To improve your CV, make a list of the most significant problems you think you would address if you worked in a particular job. (Review Exercises 8 and 26 in Chapters 1 and 3 to work on identifying key problems.)

For each potential employer problem, list your skills, knowledge, or abilities that could be useful to the solution of the problem. Next, outline the accomplishments or capabilities that demonstrate your ability to help solve this problem. Refer to your capability and accomplishment statements in Exercises 34 and 35.

Job target:_____

Employer problem:_____

_____

Which of your capabilities are useful in solving this problem?_____

_____

_____

_____

_____

Which of your accomplishments demonstrate your ability to solve this problem?_____

_____

_____

_____

_____

Job target:_____

Employer Problem:_____

_____

Which of your capabilities are useful in solving this problem?_____

_____

_____

_____

_____

Which of your accomplishments demonstrate your ability to solve this problem?_____

_____

_____

_____

_____

_____

Job target:_____

Employer problem:_____

_____

Which of your capabilities are useful in solving this problem?_____

_____

_____

_____

_____

Which of your accomplishments demonstrate your ability to solve this problem?_____

_____

_____

_____

_____

4.5 THE BEST FORMAT FOR YOU

SITUATION

Brad devoted the first part of his career to veterinary science. He earned two graduate degrees in his field, and for fifteen years managed a lab that diagnosed animal diseases. Eventually he reached the top of his career ladder and could advance no further. He decided to change careers, returning to school for an M.B.A. in business administration and human resource development.

He prepared a chronological CV listing all of his past jobs as a veterinary pathologist in chronological order. He also listed his degrees in biology and veterinary science, in addition to his newly attained M.B.A.

Brad applied for quite a few positions, but received few calls for interviews. In two interviews that he did have, the interviewer devoted most of the time to asking about his career as a veterinary pathologist and what had prompted him to make the career change. He was turned down for both positions.

Brad did not realize that those potential employers viewed him as a vet who wanted to be a business administrator—not as a business administrator who was once a vet. Of course they wouldn't want to hire him. He was a veterinarian, and they weren't hiring veterinarians.

Brad's CV was working against him. He had the skills and training to be a business administrator. He even had an extensive amount of administrative experience managing the lab. But due to an incorrect choice of format his CV communicated *veterinarian*, not *business administrator*.

JOB SEARCH PRINCIPLE TO FOLLOW

Choose the format that works best for you in each situation.

There are a variety of ways to organize the information in your CV so that it elicits the proper positive response from the employer to whom it is sent. On the following pages three different CV formats are demonstrated:

The **chronological CV** organizes your work experience by when it occurred.

The **functional CV** organizes your experience by areas of skill, avoiding a strict reliance on chronology.

The **targeted CV** aims at a specific job opportunity and organizes information more in terms of what is needed for the job than what you've done in the past.

STRATEGIC ACTIONS

✍ Exercise 38: SELECTING THE CV FORMAT

Review the CV formats on the following pages and analyze the advantages and disadvantages of each. You may also want to take the quick CV format selector quiz directly below to determine what might be the best CV format for you.

CV Format Selector Quiz

Step 1: Check any statement that pertains to you and your current job search.

A. _____ Looking for first job
B. _____ Staying in the same field as past jobs
C. _____ Job history shows real growth and development
D. _____ Changing career goals
E. _____ Past titles are highly impressive
F. _____ Name of last employer is an important consideration
G. _____ Have been absent from the job market for a while
H. _____ Want to emphasize employment history
I. _____ Want to de-emphasize dates
J. _____ Changed employers too frequently
K. _____ Skills are more impressive than work history
L. _____ Have performed a limited number of skills in past jobs
M. _____ Want to make an impressive case for a specific job target
N. _____ Very clear about job direction
O. _____ Not clear about job targets
P. _____ Only want one all-purpose CV
Q. _____ Not certain of skills and capabilities
R. _____ Willing to write a CV for each job target
S. _____ Just starting, and have limited experience
T. _____ Have skills, but not much experience

Step 2: For each item checked above, put a check next to that same item in the boxes below.

Chronological CV
(emphasizes career growth and work experience)

Advantages
B. _____ Staying in the same field as past jobs
C. _____ Job history shows real growth and development
E. _____ Past titles are highly impressive
F. _____ Name of last employer is an important consideration
H. _____ Want to emphasize employment history

Disadvantages
A. _____ Looking for first job
D. _____ Changing career goals
G. _____ Have been absent from the job market for a while
I. _____ Want to de-emphasize dates
J. _____ Changed employers too frequently

```
┌─────────────────────────────────────────────────────────────┐
│                        Functional CV                          │
│                  (emphasizes areas of skill)                  │
│                                                               │
│  Advantages                                                   │
│  A. ____   Looking for first job                              │
│  D. ____   Changing career goals                              │
│  G. ____   Have been absent from the job market for a while   │
│  J. ____   Changed employers too frequently                   │
│  K. ____   Skills are more impressive than work history       │
│                                                               │
│  Disadvantages                                                │
│  C. ____   Job history shows real growth and development      │
│  F. ____   Name of last employer is an important consideration│
│  H. ____   Want to emphasize employment history               │
│  L. ____   Have performed a limited number of skills in past jobs│
│                                                               │
└─────────────────────────────────────────────────────────────┘


┌─────────────────────────────────────────────────────────────┐
│                        Targeted CV                            │
│         (focuses on skills and supporting accomplishments for │
│                    a specific job target)                     │
│                                                               │
│  Advantages                                                   │
│  M. ____   Want to make an impressive case for a specific job target│
│  N. ____   Very clear about job direction                     │
│  R. ____   Willing to write a CV for each job target          │
│  T. ____   Have skills, but not much experience               │
│                                                               │
│  Disadvantages                                                │
│  O. ____   Not clear about job targets                        │
│  P. ____   Only want one all-purpose CV                       │
│  Q. ____   Not certain of skills and capabilities             │
│  S. ____   Just starting, and have limited experience         │
│                                                               │
└─────────────────────────────────────────────────────────────┘
```

Step 3: Review the advantages and disadvantages of each format. Put two checks next to considerations that are very important to you. Select the format that is best for you. If you are still unclear about which format to choose, try writing your CV using different formats and compare the results.

WRITING A CHRONOLOGICAL CV

The chronological CV emphasizes work experience and personal history. This CV communicates that you are *experienced* and *established* in one career area.

- Start with your most recent position and work backward, devoting the most space to recent employment. Detail only the last four or five positions of the last ten or so years. You don't need to show every position change within a given employer.
- Do not repeat details common to several positions. Stress major accomplishments and responsibilities that demonstrate your full competency to do the job.
- Keep your job target in mind, and as you describe prior positions and accomplishments, emphasize those that are most closely related to your next move up.
- If you have completed a relevant course or received a degree within the past five years, it should go at the top of the CV; otherwise, education should be listed at the bottom.
- Keep the length of your CV to one page.

CHRONOLOGICAL CV

JOHN FRENCH
45 Somerville Road
Palmerston, Warks WK3 2JP
(0834) 222 2345

WORK EXPERIENCE

1985–
Present
MORETON SYMES PLC   Birmingham

Divisional Controller

Report directly to the Financial Director. Manage cash funds. Prepare consolidated corporation tax returns for seven companies and financial review of major subsidiaries. Design and prepare a monthly sales comparison for corporate executives. Co-supervisor of finance for a £45-million company.

1984–1985 WIGMORE LYNCH PLC   Warwick

Corporate Auditor

Reported directly to the Financial Controller. Conducted operational and financial audits within the Treasurer's office and five operating divisions. Developed a report with findings and recommendations for the Managing Directors and key managerial staff of each division.

1977–1984 PRICE, MERTON & COMPANY LTD   London EC3

Senior Divisional Supervisor

Joined the professional staff as an assistant accountant. Reported directly to the partners and managers. Planned, supervised and completed numerous audit assignments.

AWARDS / ACCREDITATIONS / MEMBERSHIPS

1981   Chartered Accountant & Registered Auditor,
        Institute of Chartered Accounts in England & Wales
1977   Certified Accountant,
        Chartered Association of Certified Accountants

EDUCATION

1977   University of Warwickshire
        B.Sc. in Accountancy & Finance

Writing a Functional CV

The functional CV highlights major areas of *accomplishment* and *strength* and allows you to organize them in the order that best supports your work objectives and job targets.

- Use four or five separate paragraphs or sections, each one headlining a particular area of expertise or involvement. List functions (eg: Design, research, supervision, etc.) in order of importance, with the area most closely related to your job target at the top and described in slightly more detail.

- Within each functional area stress your accomplishments, results, or abilities most directly related to your job target.

- Know that you can include any relevant accomplishment without necessarily identifying the employment or nonemployment situation in which it took place.

- If you have completed a relevant course or received a degree within the past five years, it should go at the top of the CV; otherwise, education should be listed at the bottom.

- List a brief synopsis of your actual work experience at the bottom, giving dates, employer, and title. If you have had no work experience, or a very spotty record, leave out the employment synopsis entirely (but be prepared to talk about it at the interview).

- Keep the length of your CV to one page.

MARILYN M. GRANT
79 Cliff Court
Brighton, Sussex BN22 5RW
(0987) 677 4567

INSURANCE LAW

- Advised management of insurance underwriting firm on legality of insurance transactions.
- Studied court decisions and recommended changes in wording of insurance policies to conform with law and/or to protect company from unwarranted claims.
- Advised claims department personnel on legality of claims filed on the underwriters to insure against undue payments.
- Advised personnel engaged in drawing up legal documents such as insurance contracts and release papers.

COMPANY LAW:

- Made an extensive study of the corporate structure, including legal rights, obligations and privileges.
- Acted as agent for several corporations in various transactions.
- Studied decisions, statutes and findings of quasi-judicial bodies.

PROPERTY LAW:

Handled sale and transfer of buildings and land.
Instituted searches to establish ownership.
Drew up deeds, mortgages and leases,
Acted as trustee of property investment funds.

WORK EXPERIENCE:

1980-Present   COMMERCIAL VEHICLE UNDERWRITERS COMPANY LTD
Brighton, Sussex

Insurance Services Supervisor

EDUCATION:

1987   UNIVERSITY OF LONDON, School of Law
LL.B—Insurance Law, Company Law, Estate Planning, Taxation.

1980   UNIVERSITY OF MANCHESTER
B.A. History

WRITING A TARGETED CV

The targeted CV focuses on a clear, specific job target, listing appropriate capabilities and supporting accomplishments. Each job target requires a different CV.

- You must be clear and specific about your job target, the particular title, or occupational field you want to pursue.
- Capabilities and accomplishments must be stated briefly, each in one or two lines and be directly related to your job target.
- Your list of capabilities should answer the question, "What can you do?" Your list of accomplishments should answer the question, "What have you done?"
- Experience and education are included, but not stressed; they support the image conveyed by the CV.
- The CV should fit on one page with plenty of white space.

DAVID C. HALPERN
62 Peterfield Road
Basingstoke, Hants. RG77 4PX
(0167) 234 6789

JOB TARGET:

SALES OR MARKETING MANAGEMENT WITH AN INTERNATIONAL COMPANY

CAPABILITIES:

- Market and sell industrial and agricultural chemicals.
- Direct and co-ordinate activities concerned with research and development of new concepts, ideas and basic data on company products, services and philosophy.
- Plan and formulate aspects of research and development proposals, such as purpose of project, application of findings, cost of project and equipment requirements.
- Approve and submit feasibility proposals to management for consideration and allocation of funds.
- Negotiate contracts with consulting firms to perform studies.
- Achieve a competitive edge through effective use of know-how in product co-ordination, ship chartering and letters of credit.

ACCOMPLISHMENTS:

- Managed cost analyses pertinent to specific products and countries in relation to total consumption, pricing, competitors, market share, local production facilities, freighting and credit.
- Successfully gained market information through agents, distributors and international government agencies.
- Arranged sensitive offshore deals and reciprocal deals with competitors in Europe, the Far East and Latin America.
- Sold industrial packaging materials to blue chip companies.
- Increased market share of an industrial paper product from 27% to 31% in a six-month period.

EXPERIENCE:

1986–1994 PRODUCT MANAGER
British International Chemicals, plc., Fareham, Hampshire.

1980–1986 INTERNATIONAL SALES REPRESENTATIVE
Crown Chemicals and Coatings Ltd, Andover, Hampshire

1974–1980 SHIP'S NAVIGATOR
British Cargo Shipping Ltd, Southampton

EDUCATION:

1985 UNIVERSITY OF BRADFORD
MBA—International Business

$\boxed{4.6}$ Use Language to Your Advantage

Situation

You've read lots of other people's CVs, but now that you have to write one of your own, you're confused about how to pull it all together. Is this a narrative, a simple list of accomplishments, a third-person presentation? You're pretty clear about what you've done and what's valuable about your experience, but when you write it all down, it looks too long and wordy.

Job Search Principle to Follow

Use power language.

A good CV, just like a good advertisement, uses language that creates clear images and ideas in the reader's mind. Avoid long-winded sentences with weak beginnings and rambling conditions. Use action verbs. Eliminate extraneous information such as birth date, social security number, references, or hobbies. Generally, the simpler your CV, the easier it will be to understand.

Strategic Actions

☞ Write to persuade.

Your CV is a well-structured presentation of your capabilities and accomplishments, designed to persuade a potential employer to invite you for an interview. It is a clear, unembarrassed portrayal of yourself, presented in the best possible light.

The language of your CV must command the attention of potential employers. Begin your statements with verbs that convey actions, such as:

Programmed	Planned	Assisted	Evaluated	Developed
Administered	Produced	Negotiated	Conducted	Improved

Describe the results that you produced in your work, not just your duties and responsibilities. Every job holder has duties; successful job holders produce results.

Duty-oriented: ''Responsible for preparing customer orders, determining needs and quantities, and seeing that they were priced correctly.''

Result-oriented: "In a six-month period, served over 100 major customers and organized over ten million dollars in orders without one customer complaint."

In describing your results, use quantities (amounts and monetary values) wherever possible.

☞ Keep your CV's length to one page.

Less is more. For most job targets the best length for your CV is one page. Even if you have held numerous jobs and have several degrees, you should condense the information so that it piques the employer's interest immediately. If the information is redundant or verbose, the impact is diluted, and the employer's attention will waver.

If you have written a variety of articles or books, received a long list of honors or awards, or worked on a number of recognizable products, then you might consider preparing an addendum to your CV listing those specific items. Make it clear, however, that your CV itself ends on the first page.

☞ Eliminate unnecessary information.

After you draft your CV, go back and edit out all details that are irrelevant to your presentation or do not support your job target.

- Shorten your sentences. For example: "I was the person chosen to coordinate the college fund-raising team for homecoming week" can be restated as "Coordinated college fund-raising team."
- Eliminate repetitions. If you performed similar tasks in two or three different jobs, explain only the most recent position in detail, or change to a functional format in which you can present the information under one heading.
- Don't spell out information that is already implied. If you are a college graduate, there is no reason to describe your high school education.
- Omit company or school addresses and names of references. You can provide this information if it is requested. "References provided on request" is assumed.
- List only recent positions. If you have had a large number of past jobs, summarize the earliest with a statement like this: "1970–80. A variety of drafting positions."
- List the year or years you held a job or graduated, but omit the months and days.
- Eliminate most personal information. Employers don't need to know your weight, height, sex, marital status, health, children's names, church affiliations, social clubs, etc.

- Leave out salary history or requirements, reasons for leaving, or any information that does not present you in the best possible light.

☞ Upgrade each CV draft.

As you put together your CV, review Section 4.2 and write or rewrite the capability and accomplishment statements using the guide-lines presented above. Incorporate these statements in the paragraphs describing your work experiences and functional areas. Remember, statements should directly relate to your job target and the employer's needs.

Have one or two others review and critique each draft of your CV for content, spelling, and grammar. Delete any unnecessary information. Make sure that every statement supports your assertion that you can produce high-quality results for the prospective employer.

✍ Exercise 39: WRITING THE CV

Use the following pages to write a draft of your CV. Find the pages for the CV format you selected and enter your personal information into the different CV sections. Use additional paper as needed.

When writing the descriptions of your work history, functional areas, capabilities, and accomplishments, follow the guidelines in this chapter. Focus your descriptions on specific, quantifiable results that directly communicate to a potential employer that you are the right person for the job (see Section 4.2). Use effective CV language, and do not include unnecessary information. Review your draft to see how you can condense and improve it.

CHRONOLOGICAL CV—DRAFT

(Name and Address) _____
_____
_____
(Phone)   _____

JOB TARGET (We recommend that you use "job target" or "objectives" on the Targeted CV only. Use your cover letter to focus the reader's attention.)

_____

WORK EXPERIENCE
(Start with your most recent job and work backward in time.)

(Dates)_____ (Job Title)_____
(Employer) _____ (City/Town) _____

(Supporting

Accomplishments) _____

_____

_____

_____

_____

_____

(Dates)_____ (Job Title)_____

(Employer)_____ (City/Town) _____

(Supporting   _____

Accomplishments) _____

_____

_____

_____

_____

(Dates)_____ (Job Title)_____

(Employer)_____ (City/Town) _____

(Supporting   _____

Accomplishments) _____

_____

_____

_____

_____

_____

EDUCATION

(Dates)_____ (School)_____ (City/Town) _____

(Degree)_____ (Major)_____

(Supporting   _____

Accomplishments) _____

_____

_____

(Dates)_____ (School)_____ _____ (City/Town)_____

(Degree)_____ (Major)____ _____

(Supporting   _____

Accomplishments) _____

                 _____

                 _____

OTHER SUPPORTING INFORMATION (Include any brief additional information that supports your contention that you are the right person for the job: affiliations/associations, publications, volunteer experience, military history, etc.)

_____

_____

_____

_____

_____

_____

FUNCTIONAL CV—DRAFT

(Name and Address) _____

                   _____

                   _____

(Phone)   _____

JOB TARGET (We recommend that you use "job target" or "objectives" on the Target CV only. Use your cover letter to focus the reader's attention.)

_____

FUNCTION TITLE:_____

Achievements or results you have produced in this functional area:

_____

_____

_____

_____

_____

_____

FUNCTION TITLE:_____
Achievements or results you have produced in this functional area:

_____
_____
_____
_____

WORK EXPERIENCE (Start with your most recent job and work backward.)

(Dates)_____ (Job Title)_____

(Employer)_____ (City/Town) _____

(Dates)_____ (Job Title)_____

(Employer)_____ (City/Town) _____

(Dates)_____ (Job Title)_____

(Employer)_____ (City/Town) _____

EDUCATION

(Dates)_____ (School)_____ (City/Town) _____

(Degree)_____ (Major)_____

(Supporting _____

Accomplishments) _____

_____

_____

(Dates)_____ (School)_____ (City/Town) _____

(Degree)_____ (Major)_____

(Supporting _____

Accomplishments) _____

_____

_____

OTHER SUPPORTING INFORMATION (Include any additional brief information that supports your contention that you are the right person for the job: affiliations/associations, publications, volunteer experience, military history, etc.)

_____
_____

_____

_____

_____

TARGETED CV—DRAFT

(Name and Address) _____

_____

_____

(Phone) _____

JOB TARGET (a very specific objective)

_____

CAPABILITIES (what you can do or could do in the performance of the job target)

- _____
- _____
- _____
- _____
- _____

ACCOMPLISHMENTS (what you have done that demonstrates your ability to produce results in your job target area)

- _____
- _____
- _____
- _____
- _____

WORK EXPERIENCE (Start with your most recent job and work backward.)

(Dates)_____ (Job Title)_____

(Employer)_____ (City/Town) _____

(Dates)_____ (Job Title)_____

(Employer)_____ (City/Town) _____

(Dates)_____ (Job Title)_____

(Employer)_____ (City/Town) _____

EDUCATION

(Dates)_____   (School)_____   (City/Town)_____
                   (Degree)_____   (Major)_____
(Supporting   _____
Accomplishments) _____
                   _____
                   _____

(Dates)_____ (School)_____   (City/Town) _____
                   (Degree)_____   (Major)_____
(Supporting   _____
Accomplishments) _____
                   _____
                   _____

OTHER SUPPORTING INFORMATION (Include any additional brief information that supports your contention that you are the right person for the job: affiliations/associations, publications, volunteer experience, military history, etc.)

_____

_____

_____

_____

_____

4.7 MAKE A FIRST-CLASS PRESENTATION

SITUATION

You've done your homework, distilled the information about your past in a way that focuses on the future. You've organized your CV to make the maximum impact. Now that you've said all the right things, how do you present them?

JOB SEARCH PRINCIPLE TO FOLLOW

Make a first-class presentation.

The way your CV looks—how it's laid out and printed—communicates as clearly as the way you dress for an interview. Your CV should look professional, to the point, and attractive. Take the extra time and effort—or money—to make a first-class presentation, fully edited, carefully proofread, and attractive.

STRATEGIC ACTIONS

☞ Use the flash test.

An employer decides whether or not your CV is of interest in the first three or four seconds, the same way you might scan the pages of a newspaper or magazine to decide which articles or advertisements are worth reading. Just as your appearance is critical to the success of an interview, the appearance of your CV is critical in capturing the attention of a potential employer.

Make your CV attractive to the eye. Here are a few tips:

- Leave plenty of white space to accent the content of your CV and make it easier to read. Use wide margins and double spacing between major sections.

- Use a bulleted format instead of traditional paragraphs. Bulleted statements are easier to read than long paragraphs.

- Highlight key information in boldface or by underlining (but don't go overboard).

- Produce your CV on a high-quality computer or word processor with a laser printer.

- Use quality paper stock. Choose white, ivory, buff, or off-white. Avoid tinted paper.

☞ Store your CV on a computer.

Personal computers eliminate much of the labor in creating a hard-hitting and attractive CV. Word processing programs allow you to easily store multiple versions on disk for future printings.

Intelligent CV writing software extends the capability of a word processor with choices in vocabulary, format, and layout design. *The Perfect CV Computer Kit*, by this author, is designed to offer you all the features of a word processor, CV consultant, and layout designer. See page 207.

If you do not have a computer or word processor at home or in the office, you can easily get access to one through libraries, counseling centers, community colleges, or copy shops.

4.8 SPECIAL CIRCUMSTANCES

I'm in my fifties, and my CV really shows my age. I am afraid that this might turn off potential employers.

Never forget that the purpose of a CV is to get you interviews. It must clearly and concisely communicate that you are the right person for the job. If dates of past employment would deter an employer from calling you in for an interview, omit them. Use the targeted or functional CV format to emphasize your wealth of knowledge and ability rather than your past history.

I just graduated from college and don't have a lot of experience. How do I make employers take me seriously?

Employers will take you seriously if your own knowledge, skills, and experience can create value for others. (Review the Universal Hiring Rule in Section 1.6.) Consider projects you completed in school, organizations in which you participated or held positions of responsibility, volunteer work, or other nonpaid work experience. Use the targeted or functional formats that don't depend on past experience. Stress qualitative factors and leadership roles. And don't be afraid to sound self-assured.

Should I put my education at the beginning of the CV or toward the end?

Where you list your educational background depends on how important it is in your making a strong impression on a potential employer. If you are seeking a job in which a college degree is an important requirement, or if you are a recent graduate and you lack direct work experience, list education at the beginning of your CV. Otherwise, it can be placed at the end.

Should I list references on my CV?

References should be typed on a separate sheet of paper and presented to an employer when requested. Don't supply your reference list in advance of an interview. You don't want an employer to start checking up on you before you have a chance to make a strong impression in person. If you were referred to the employer by a mutual friend or business acquaintance, mention this person's name in your cover letter.

Many CVs include "References will be furnished upon request" as the last statement. Don't employers assume that you will give them references if asked?

Yes, they do. Every inch of space is precious; don't waste it on unnecessary statements.

How important is it to include an objective?

We recommend that you save the objective for the cover letter. By putting it at the top of the CV you run the risk that it is either too vague ("any position that will maximize my skills and experience") or too specific ("landing-gear design"). A targeted CV is the exception.

I'm a homemaker. What can I say on my CV if I've spent the last fifteen years raising a family?

Whether two years or fifteen, to spend time rearing children is a positive choice. Many home managing skills and qualities are applicable in the workplace. Highlight work you have done in community, school, or other volunteer projects. Consider using the targeted or functional format to stress the capabilities and personal qualities that will create value for the employer. As with any CV, make sure you address the needs of the employer in a way that communicates that you are the right person for the job.

The chronological format works best for me; however, I also have skills that I've developed outside of paid work experience. Can I combine the chronological and functional CVs?

Yes. A "combination" CV is particularly useful if you have experience in a job target area in which you want to show your career growth (chronological) and an area of skill or capability that you developed outside of your work experience, at school, at home, etc.

On a chronological CV, do all positions listed have to be paid work experience?

No. You may include volunteer experience or participation in civic, school, or other groups. The important point is that you held a position of responsibility in which you contributed value, produced results, or gained skills that are transferable to your job target area.

How about "gaps" in my work history—times when I was between jobs or, like now, when I've been looking for a job for an embarrassingly long time?

You can take some liberties with dates. The easiest is to simply round off from months to years, e.g.: 1987 to 1992 would not automatically reveal that you left your last job in June 1992. Many people list their last job as "1987 to present," which can be "explained" by the idea that this was true when the CV was prepared. However you play with the dates, be prepared to explain the gap in the interview. When you fill out a formal application, you will probably be forced to give exact months of employment.

In anticipation of a gap, you might want to set yourself up in a freelance position or as a consultant. Then you can describe yourself as "self-employed."

References

The Perfect CV Tom Jackson (Piatkus)

The Perfect CV Computer Kit Tom Jackson and Bill Buckingham. (KIPS, see page 207).

Marketing Yourself Dorothy Leeds (Piatkus)

Power Cover Letters

A powerful cover letter for your CV is one of your best marketing tools. It communicates your value directly to the employer in terms that he can understand. It paves the way for your CV.

The secret of writing a cover letter, or any business communication, is to focus on and request a particular outcome—in this case, an interview. Your cover letter should address a particular person by name, demonstrate that you know something about that employer, and show how your skills would meet her needs.

A good cover letter can demonstrate not only your interest in the employer's present opportunities, but your abilities as a communicator. Use your cover letter to demonstrate your uniqueness and value and, of course, to ask for a meeting.

Key Job Search Principles

5.1 Use a cover letter to personalize your CV communication.

5.2 Address your cover letter to a particular person, by name.

5.3 Demonstrate your knowledge of the employer.

5.4 Ask for a meeting.

5.1 A Companion to Your CV

SITUATION

Imagine that you are the employer. You were notified today that your company just signed a large contract with an international client. It's well known that your company was being considered for the contract—all the local newspapers ran feature articles about the opportunity.

Now you need to increase your staff quickly to handle the extra work. It's your job to review over a thousand CVs that have been received during the last few weeks.

Just about everyone sent a CV and standard cover letter saying: *"I am interested in working for your company. Please accept my CV ... "* All of those letters sound the same, and after a while you don't bother reading them.

But one letter stands out. Its sender took the initiative to describe what she knew about the employer and the international client. Her letter added to the value of her CV by pointing out her specific capabilities and accomplishments that would relate to the needs of the new project.

JOB SEARCH PRINCIPLE TO FOLLOW

Use a cover letter to personalize your CV communication.

Even though you already may have targeted your CVs for particular employers or jobs, you should still write a customized cover letter. A cover letter is a personal communication, generally typed on letterhead stationery, that focuses on a specific employment situation and lets the employer see how your experience and CV relate to his particular need. By taking the time to prepare an individual cover letter for each CV you mail out, you vastly increase your chances for obtaining an interview with the right person in the right company.

STRATEGIC ACTIONS

✍ Exercise 40: COVER LETTER SELECTION

What follows are characteristics of both a limp cover letter and a powerful cover letter. Even though we've given our hand away as to which we recommend, go through the process of reading the comments before each, and check to determine which type of letter you should write.

The Limp Cover Letter

_____ I really don't know to whom I am writing this letter, but that's OK. It can be read by anyone who sees it.

_____ All I need to say in the letter is that I am enclosing my CV. The employer can look at it and if he likes what he sees, he can give me a call.

_____ I have no idea what the employer does or needs at this time. Anyway, it's not necessary to talk about that in my cover letter.

_____ I don't have to write about what I have to offer the employer. She can figure that out from my CV.

_____ I'll tell the employer to give me a call to set up an interview, and I'll just wait for the phone to ring.

The Power Cover Letter

_____ I want to know the specific person who will be reading my letter and responding to it.

_____ I want the employer to know that I have taken the initiative to learn about his organization and to think about how I can assist him.

_____ I will make sure the employer knows about the specific aspects of my CV that directly relate to her needs by pointing them out in my letter.

_____ I want the employer to know how I plan to follow through on my letter. I don't want to waste time sitting around waiting for the phone to ring. I will take the next step.

Which letter do you want to prepare?

A Limp Cover Letter

Our minds go blank when we read a form letter—or a letter that is just a formality. A limp cover letter is a meaningless communication that says nothing about you. Most likely it will not arouse an employer's interest in interviewing you.

JOHN SMITH
17 Westcliff Avenue
Ramsgate, Kent CT2 4NN

Date

Lakeside Shopping Centre
Security Office
Carswell Road
Ramsgate
Kent CT22 5TA

To Whom It May Concern

I am responding to the advertisement you placed in the *Ramsgage Times* for the Security Administrator position. Please accept my CV for this position.

I am available to meet you at your convenience. You can reach me on 0123 344 356. If I am not available, please leave a message on my answering machine.

Thank you for your consideration. I look forward to speaking with you.

Yours faithfully,

John Smith

A POWERFUL COVER LETTER

The power cover letter is an opportunity for you to present yourself to an employer in a way that captures the employer's attention. The tone of the letter should be:

Professional AND warm and friendly

Interesting to read AND short and to the point

Enthusiastic and assertive BUT not pushy or begging for a position

---

SHIRLEY WARNER
17 Rochester Road
Ramsgate, Kent CT5 9OP

Date

Richard Brook, Manager
Lakeside Shopping Centre
Carswell Road
Ramsgate
Kent CT22 5TA

Dear Mr Brook

As you are aware, the changing demographics and the rise in the crime rate in the Ramsgate area have presented the Lakeside Shopping Centre with a number of new security and economic problems that directly affect its future development. For the last 10 years, we have relied on the shopping centre as a cornerstone of the local community and are concerned that a number of the key shops will close down if the situation does not improve.

For the last ten years, I have been an active community organiser, gathering local support in developing projects and finding the resources to help make the community a better place in which to live.

Increasing security in the shopping centre is one answer to the complex problem that the centre faces. Improving community support for Lakeside is critical to the long-term survival of the centre. I have the background, experience and innovative thinking to provide you with a long-term plan for security at the shopping centre.

Please accept my CV in application for your Security Administration position. I will call you early next week to discuss these ideas further and to arrange a time for us to meet. Thank you for your consideration.

Your sincerely,

Shirley Warner

5.2 WRITE TO A REAL PERSON

SITUATION

You are writing a cover letter to accompany your CV and you do not have the name of a person in the company to whom to send the letter. You could send the letter to the personnel office and address it "To Whom It May Concern." But how do you know that your letter will get past a secretary's desk? And whom will you contact to follow up?

JOB SEARCH PRINCIPLE TO FOLLOW

Address your cover letter to a particular person, by name.

Mass-market CV mailings receive very poor response. In a competitive job market you do far better targeting particular people by name. Send your cover letter and CV to the person who can make the hiring decision, not necessarily to the personnel department. Finding the right person to contact will take you a long way toward establishing the communications you need to build the relationships you want.

STRATEGIC ACTIONS

☞ Select the "decision maker" who can hire you. In most cases this is not someone in personnel but a manager in the organization, the person for whom you will work if you get the job.

If you do not know the person's name, call the employer to ask, and be persistent. It may take two or three phone calls. If you are asked why you want to know, don't say that you are looking for a job; say that you have some information to submit and want to ensure that it gets to the right person. If you still can't get through, try calling the president's office and asking for the name of the manager who runs the department in which you are interested.

Before sending your letter, make sure you have the correct spelling of both name and title.

☞ Other approaches for getting names:

There are a variety of resources for obtaining the names of key people in a given organization.

- Call someone from your contact network who knows the company and can refer you to a specific person.

- At your library, look in a business directory. For examples see page 200.

- Obtain a copy of the directory of a professional association in your job target area.

- If you know the general area or title of the function, call the company switchboard and ask for the name ("I have some material to send the training director, would you please give me the party's name and extension?").

5.3 DEMONSTRATE YOUR VALUE

SITUATION

Your CV does a great job of describing your skills and ability to produce results, but it doesn't fully address the specific needs of the employer. You have tailored your CV as much as you can, but you still need to convey your specific ideas about what you can do for the employer. This is a job for the cover letter.

JOB SEARCH PRINCIPLE TO FOLLOW

Demonstrate your knowledge of the employer.

Demonstrating that you know something about your targeted company also shows that you care enough to take the time to do the job right. Find out about the employer's needs, products, contracts, flow of business, and competition. Address ways you feel you can contribute to the company. The extra time invested will pay dividends for you.

STRATEGIC ACTIONS

☞ Use a strong opening.

Get right to the point in the opening paragraph of your letter. If you were referred by someone known to the employer or an authority in the field, name the reference in the first sentence. It will make the employer more receptive to what follows. For example:

"Harold Becker at *Newsworld* suggested that I write to you about an approach to reporting local news that I developed . . ."

"Your name came up at the Cornell Media Conference as a leader in imaginative programming . . ."

"Joann Hanson, a mutual friend, suggested that I contact you regarding your new literacy program . . ."

☞ Demonstrate your knowledge of the situation.

The body of your cover letter presents the information you want the employer to consider immediately, even before turning to your CV. This is the place to highlight concisely your knowledge of the employer's business concerns and how you can help.

The more you understand about the employer and his or her work situation, the more valuable you are. If the body of your letter is strong enough, the employer may consider hiring you immediately. For example:

"Your department has entered a stage of product development to which I feel I can make a contribution . . ."

"An article in October's *Builder* identified your firm as an innovator in modular design. I thought that several of my ideas could assist you to establish further your position as a leader in this field."

"As you will see from my CV, my seven years of experience as creative director at the Gruening Agency has prepared me to make a direct and immediate contribution to your current Rival campaign."

"My CV highlights my successes in improving line production by 30% in two years. I feel that my accomplishments in this area and in interdepartmental quality control have prepared me to make an equal contribution to your organization."

✍ Exercise 41: OFFERING SOLUTIONS

Answer the following questions to help organize the content of your power cover letter. Use your answers to compose the opening and body of the letter.

What is the problem or concern that I can help solve?_____

_____

_____

How can I assist the employer immediately?_____

_____

_____

_____

What have I accomplished that demonstrates that I can contribute?

_____

_____

_____

_____

How will the employer benefit from hiring me?_____

_____

_____

_____

_____

5.4 Ask for a Meeting

SITUATION

You usually end your cover letters asking the employer to contact you: "I am available to meet with you at your convenience. You can contact me at . . ." But the employer rarely calls.

JOB SEARCH PRINCIPLE TO FOLLOW

Ask for a meeting.

Once you have put together a sharp CV and a focused cover letter addressed to the right person, it is time to ask for a meeting. Make a clear and unequivocal request at the end of your cover letter.

After you have requested a meeting, follow up by phone within a few days of receipt of your letter by the employer.

STRATEGIC ACTIONS

☞ End your letter with a call to action.

Avoid vague endings that leave the initiative and the interview up to the employer. To arrange the interview is up to you. Do not ask, "Please contact me . . . ," but state, "I will contact you . . ."

You seized the initiative by sending out a compelling cover letter and CV. Now let the employer know that your time is valuable too. If the decision maker believes you can help solve her problem, she will agree to see you. For example:

"I'd like to stop by next Tuesday or Wednesday to show you copies of my promotional ideas. I know we can both benefit greatly by meeting. Please expect my call early next week to set up the time."

"I hope we can get together so that I can show you the working model of my program. I'll call your secretary when I arrive in town next week to set up a date."

SAMPLE COVER LETTER

BARBARA WILEY
26 Park Drive
Billericay, Essex CH1 3FF

Date

Kevin Davis, FCA
Davis, Davis and Simpson
134 North Street
Chelmsford
Essex CM1 3RR

Dear Mr. Davis,

Janet Lee from Grant, Lee and Lowery mentioned that your firm is looking for people to prepare personal and company tax returns on a temporary, full-time basis over the next few months.

I believe that I am an ideal candidate for this position. My credentials include a B.A. in accounting from Colchester College and three years' tax preparation experience with Grant, Lee and Lowery. The last five years have been primarily devoted to raising a family; however I have worked with Accord Accountants preparing personal tax returns. I have kept up with the changes in the tax laws through a variety of college and adult education courses.

I pride myself in offering a quality service to clients and in maintaining standards of thoroughness and accuracy, while exploring ways to minimise a client's tax liability.

Enclosed is a copy of my CV for your review. I will be in touch with you early next week to arrange a time for us to meet. I look forward to meeting you and discussing how I can assist your organisation.

Your sincerely,

Barbara Wiley

SAMPLE COVER LETTER

JEFF LONG
17 Coney Drive
Woking, Surrey GU7 8YU

Date

Joan Babcock
H&T Productions Ltd
14 Park Street
Windsor
Berks WN1 3DF

Dear Ms. Babcock,

The article in *Video Today* identified your company as one of the leaders in industrial training videos in the country. Your great success and growth in business has been attributed to the quality of your work in serving your client's needs. I have had the opportunity of viewing your video series on industrial safety standards for Hemway Controls and I am impressed with your standards of video production.

As your business grows to meet increasing demands in the industry, you will need ways to streamline your production capacity. I would like to meet with you to discuss ways in which I can help you achieve this objective.

My CV highlights by background and accomplishments in video production, including:

- Five years' experience using strong conceptual, writing and production skills.
- A thorough understanding of graphic design and computer simulations.
- An ability to produce quality programmes within tight deadlines and budget constraints.
- Direct experience with directing and acting in videos I have produced.

I will be in Berkshire next Thursday and Friday and I would like to take the opportunity to talk to you and show you some samples of my work. I will be in touch with your office at the end of this week to arrange a time to meet.

Thank you for your consideration. I look forward to the opportunity to become part of your dynamic team.

Your sincerely,

Jeff Long

SAMPLE COVER LETTER

GEMMA JONES
30 Leamington Avenue
Surbiton, Surrey KT2 5CV

Date

James Pereira, Managing Director
Williams and Bell Advertising, Ltd.
308b Baker Street
London WC3B 2RS

Dear Mr Pereira,

At the National Association meeting in Harrogate last week, our mutual friend and colleague, Bill Franklin, informed me that you are interested in someone with credentials like mine for your new Sony account. W & B's record of financial and creative performance has long impressed me and I am excited by the possibility of our joining forces.

At General Electronics, I assumed full responsibility for creating, co-ordinating and budgeting all advertising and sales promotion for household appliances, including bottom line interfacing on our £4 million account with BBD&O. I am confident that my background and expertise, summarised in the enclosed CV, equip me particularly well to run the Sony account.

I would be pleased to meet with you next month to explore the matter further. I will call you next week to arrange a mutually convenient date.

I look forward to meeting you.

Your sincerely,

Gemma Jones

✍ Exercise 42: COVER LETTER DRAFT

Use this form to draft a trial cover letter. Follow the guidelines in this chapter for each section of your letter. Always look for ways to make your letter more powerful and to communicate your value so that it has greater impact when read. After you have typed it have someone in your personal support network critique and proofread your letter before mailing it.

(Your name and address) _____
_____
_____

_____ **(Date)**

_____ **(Address your letter to a particular**
_____ **person, by name.)**
_____

Dear_____:

(Use a strong opening that gets right to the point—Section 5.3.)

_____
_____
_____
_____
_____

(Demonstrate your knowledge of the company and address ways you feel you can contribute to its needs—Section 5.3.)

_____
_____
_____
_____
_____
_____

(End your letter with a call to action. Ask for a meeting—Section 5.4.)

_____

_____

_____

_____

_____

                               Sincerely,

                    _____

References

Cover Letters that Will Get You the Job You Want Stanley Wynett (Better Way Books)
The Perfect CV Tom Jackson (Piatkus)

Getting Inside for Interviews

Your actions in a job search can be divided into two categories: "internal"—research, targeting, CV preparation, and networking; and "external"—talking to specific employers, obtaining interviews, taking interviews, and negotiating for the job. It is in external action that the promotion and legwork you've done pays off. It takes courage and persistence to move from the internal world to the external, to revise your wishes and commitments in light of the face-to-face communication with the people who can hire you.

It is important as you take external action to remember that employers need you as much as you need them. They aren't hiring people to be charitable or social-minded. They're hiring qualified candidates because they feel that by so doing they can increase profits for their organization or benefits to their constituencies. As a job candidate, you have as much to offer an employer as the employer has to offer you. As you bear this in mind, and consider your assets with pride, your demeanor will gain strength and credibility.

Key Job Search Principles

6.1 Employers need you as much as you need them.

6.2 Stay on the case.

6.3 Break the phone barrier.

6.4 Be creative.

6.1 IT'S A TWO-WAY STREET

SITUATION

After an extended period of time in the job search process you may find your self-esteem going a little flat. You've given the employer all the power: the power to reject your CV, to not respond to your brilliant cover letters, to ignore your request for an interview, or to not get back to you after you've had one. You may find yourself feeling more "needy" and less able. You may begin to believe that you need the job more than the employer needs you. Don't.

JOB SEARCH PRINCIPLE TO FOLLOW

Employers need you as much as you need them.

Always consider the job search as a negotiation between equals. It may not feel that way to you when you're in a tight job market or between jobs. It may seem that the employer has all the cards. However, employers require good talent to produce the performances, products, and revenues they need to survive.

Review the power phrases on your CV. Role-play with friends. Do whatever it takes to reaffirm and refamiliarize yourself with your strengths and capabilities before contacting employers for interviews.

STRATEGIC ACTIONS

☞ In Section 1.6, we discussed the Universal Hiring Rule: *Any employer will hire any individual as long as the employer is convinced that the hiring will bring more value than it costs.*

It takes people to create value. A natural resource is worthless until someone discovers a use for it and converts it to that use. A machine is worthless unless someone can operate it. A database is worthless unless someone can manipulate its contents and interpret the data retrieved from it.

An employer depends on his employees to get the job done cost-effectively.

Review the sections of this book listed below. If you've already read through a section and followed its strategic actions, rethink your work. Are there other strategies you can follow? Is there another way to communicate the value you offer with greater strength?

If you have not read through these sections, take time to do so now.

They contain the key elements that will enable you to make contact with prospective employers and turn interviews into offers.

Check if Completed
- [ ] Section 1.6   The Universal Hiring Rule
- [ ] Section 2.4   Job Seeking Is a Worthy Activity
- [ ] Section 3.2   Create a Job
- [ ] Section 4.2   A Value-Added CV
- [ ] Section 4.4   The "All-Purpose" CV Is Obsolete
- [ ] Section 5.3   Demonstrate Your Value

☞ Analyze your past job(s)—whether full-time, part-time, or volunteer—and isolate the accomplishments that have created tangible value for previous employers. See if you can put a sterling figure to this value.

☞ Consider what you can do to contribute value to a future employer's operation. How can you increase sales, reduce costs, expedite new products or markets, etc.? Try to quantify this.

6.2   STAY ON THE CASE

SITUATION

You've carefully thought out your job target, researched potential employers, written a dynamic CV, contacted job placement firms, and sent out your CV to dozens of employers. You've let it be known that you're available. What more can you do?

JOB SEARCH PRINCIPLE TO FOLLOW

Stay on the case.

Finding a new job or changing your career direction is a fundamentally important challenge. Its outcome determines much about the quality of your future. Do not take the process lightly, and do not turn over the responsibility for it to search firms or counselors. Be willing to set your own direction and pursue it relentlessly stage by stage. At times the horizon will look bleak. You may experience rejection and unreturned phone calls, and come to feel there's really nothing out there for you.

    Don't give up. Continue to take the steps necessary to target more closely, to develop more contacts, and to turn interviews into offers. Set daily and weekly work targets. Organize a plan. Work in teams with others. Rejections are a part of every job campaign. Even the best job search yields a series of nos before the great big YES! Don't let the nos slow you down.

STRATEGIC ACTIONS

☞ Initiate contact with employers.

Narrow down your top employer prospects and select the ones you want to target for interviews. Focus on initiating contact with these employers, doing whatever it takes to stimulate their interest in meeting with you.

Here is an organized approach to pursuing interview meetings.

1. Identify each potential employer and the person you want to meet.
2. Send a power cover letter that clearly states your interest in the employer and the value that you can contribute. Enclose a copy of your CV.
3. Follow up your letter five days later by contacting the person by phone. Keep calling until you reach him.
4. When contact is made, stress the prime value you communicated in your letter. Ask for a meeting.
5. If you get an objection, meet it and repeat your request for a personal meeting.
6. If the answer is still no, thank the employer for his time, send a new follow-up letter in six weeks, and try again. Be persistent, but not obnoxious.
7. After three turndowns, consider putting the case on the back burner.

Direct your campaign at those employers to whom you have something very distinct and specific to communicate: "Here's a problem or concern that you face, and here's how I can help." Stay with the contacting phase until you are convinced that your value has been recognized.

☞ Keep track of all your contacts.

Use the Employer Contact Log on p. 137. Copy this form, or make up your own, for each employer on your list. Review your notes on that employer and write a summary of his or her needs and the value you offer.

Keep a record of all contacts with each employer. On a weekly basis, review your log to follow up on your contacts. It is easy to make initial contact, experience rejection, and cease your efforts with that employer. If you are convinced that you can make a real contribution to the company, don't give up. The employer needs you as much as you need the employer. It may take a few attempts to get the employer to listen, so be persistent.

☞ Set daily targets.

Review the strategic actions for scheduling your time in Section 2.2. It is vital that you set goals for yourself, organize your time, create a daily agenda, and stick to it until your goals are achieved. This keeps you focused on the tasks at hand and provides a sense of accomplishment when you see that your goals are being met. It's easy to procrastinate or to let discouragement prevent you from taking action to produce tangible results. By putting your intentions in writing you are making a commitment to action.

Make copies of the Daily Log on page 138 and use it (or your own form) to set your targets for the day, both in your job search and in your other pursuits. At the end of each day take fifteen minutes to list everything you accomplished that day and to plan your activities for the next.

✍ Exercise 43: EMPLOYER CONTACT LOG

Business/Organization:_____

Person to contact:_____

Secretary's name:_____ **Phone:**_____ **Ext.:**_____ **Fax:**_____

Key information about the business:_____

_____

_____

_____

Contributions and value you offer:_____

_____

_____

_____

Contact Log

Date	Contact (Phone, Letter, Fax, etc.)	Follow-Up Action
_____	_____	_____
_____	_____	_____
_____	_____	_____
_____	_____	_____
_____	_____	_____
_____	_____	_____
_____	_____	_____
_____	_____	_____
_____	_____	_____

Comments:_____

_____

_____

_____

_____

✍ Exercise 44: DAILY LOG

For:_____
(date)

Goals for Today:

To:_____
To:_____
To:_____
_____
_____

Time	Planned Actions	Done	Further Actions to Take
____	_____	____	_____
____	_____	____	_____
____	_____	____	_____
____	_____	____	_____
____	_____	____	_____
____	_____	____	_____

Accomplishments/Recap:_____
_____
_____
_____

6.3 Break the Phone Barrier

Situation

You've sent off your CV and cover letter. In closing the cover letter, you wrote that you would call to set up an interview. It's now time to make that call. You are reluctant to pick up the phone. You feel nervous. What if you say the wrong thing and ruin your chances of being considered?

Job Search Principle to Follow

Break the phone barrier.

The telephone is your greatest ally. It holds the power of enhanced communication and the opportunity to open up at any moment possibilities that were previously closed. And yet many of us suffer in silence. We hope, we fear, we conjecture, and we blame the system. We make assumptions about why we haven't heard from the people to whom we posted our CVs, and we put off the call that would let us find out. In short, we catch "phonophobia" in the worst way, and our relentless job search is put on hold.

A powerful telephone campaign is the best answer to a difficult job search.

Strategic Actions

☞ The follow-up call:

Send your CV and a well-written cover letter (see Chapter 5) before calling a prospective employer. Once you've initiated contact by mail, you can start your phone conversation by referring to your letter. The letter itself has paved the way for making a good impression on the employer.

The "cold call" strategy, i.e., using the telephone *before* sending a preparatory letter and CV, puts you under pressure to make a good impression immediately. But it has the advantage of speed and directness; since there has been no letter, the employer has few preconceived notions to get in the way. This approach also has the advantage that if the contact doesn't end up in a meeting or interview, you can always send a letter and CV to start the cycle again.

☞ Telephone tactics:

Note: These tactics apply to your response to both an advertised position and an unadvertised position. In both cases you want to try to have a conversation with the person who will make the decision to hire, not a personnel representative. In the case of an advertised position you might want to do both—go through channels and make a direct approach after you uncover the hiring person's name.

- Organize your message in advance so that it's clear, concise, coherent, and confident.
- Remember that your goal is to schedule an interview—not to engage in a conversation about your qualifications.
- Reread everything that you have in your files about the organization.
- Make some notes of key words and phrases that you feel will help you communicate. You don't want to read your presentation, but notes will help you remember what to say.
- Practice what you plan to say in a telephone role-play in advance.
- Keep your opening presentation to one minute or less.
- Be sure you know the name and title of the person you want to reach.
- Identify yourself. If you are following up a letter, say so, and restate the reason you feel the employer should see you.
- Once you have established the employer's interest, get to the point: "The reason I'm calling is to see if we can set up a short meeting. I'd like to show you some examples of my work and to find out more about what you are doing. Can we meet tomorrow afternoon?"

☞ Getting by the secretary:

The main hurdle to clear in reaching the employer is convincing his or her secretary to put you through. This can be a major obstacle when you are responding to an advertisement, since many other people will be trying to reach the employer too. You may be passed on to the personnel department.

- If the secretary answers, ask directly and positively for the person you want. "This is Lillian Fisher. I'd like to talk with Susan Olsen, please."

- If the secretary hesitates for a moment, maintain your silence. If he asks, "What's this in reference to?" don't become defensive or apologetic. State the purpose of your call in more or less technical terms: "I'd like to discuss the demographics of your market research study" or "I'd like to get some information about your new outreach program."

- If the secretary then asks, "May I help you?" don't fight it. "Perhaps you can . . . could you tell me when I might be able to reach Ms. Olsen for a brief discussion?" Or, "Yes, I want to arrange a meeting with Ms. Olsen about some technical matters. Will she be in next Tuesday at four o'clock?"

- If you are unsuccessful, don't show irritation. Insist politely, "When would be a good time to call back?"

- Call after five o'clock. Many secretaries leave at 5:00 P.M., and the bosses often stay longer.

- Don't rely on leaving a message and getting a return phone call. Most busy employers will not return phone calls from people unknown to them. Stay with the initiative and find a good time to call back.

- Be persistent. It will generally take several phone calls to get through.

✍ Exercise 45: THE PHONE PITCH

Use the following format to make your own outline of the points you want to include in your telephone conversations. Set up your first six calls, then pick up the phone and go! Make as many calls as you can at one sitting. After each call, write down the results and the next actions you plan to take.

Before the call:

Who you are calling? _____

What do you want to happen as a result of this call?_____

_____

_____

What points do you plan to make about the value you offer?

_____

_____

_____

_____

How are you going to state your request to the employer?_____ _

_____ _____

After the call:
What were the results of the call?_____

_____

_____

_____

What actions do you need to take next to further the relationship with this employer?

_____

_____

_____

_____

✍ Exercise 46: OVERCOMING OBJECTIONS

There are dozens of reasons why the employer might not want to see you. One of the biggest is that he is not convinced of the value in meeting with you. He thinks it would be a waste of time. It is essential that you communicate a clear purpose for setting up the meeting, that you are not asking, "What can you do for me?", but rather stating, "Here's what I can do for you. Let's talk about it."

Employer objections are natural and unavoidable, but these objections should not stop you. The way to overcome objections is to anticipate them, to acknowledge them, and to be ready with positive ways to overcome them.

- When an employer "can't see you now," ask for a future date, or ask for someone else who can meet with you.

- When the employer says that she is not hiring new people, tell her that you are not looking to fill a position, you want to talk about how you can create value for her business and want to discuss employment only if she is convinced of this value.

- When you first hear the objection, "get it" ("I understand how you would think that") then offer another possibility ("I think I have an approach that will give you another way of looking at it").

Mastering the Obstacle Course:
In a telephone role-play, have your partner read each of the following objections. Repeat each to indicate that you really heard it, and then communicate another interpretation.

Employer: "You're overqualified."

You:_____

_____

Employer: "We were looking for someone a little younger [older]."

You: _____

_____

Employer: "All hiring is done by Personnel."

You: _____

_____

Employer: "We need someone with more experience in the field."

You: _____

_____

Employer: "We're cutting back right now. Why don't you call back in three months?"

You: _____

_____

Employer: "We'll let you know in a few weeks."

You: _____

_____

Employer: "I'll be on a business trip for the next two weeks."

You: _____

_____

Employer: "The person in charge of hiring is not around."

You: _____

_____

Employer: "We're looking for someone with more practical experience."

You: _____

_____

Employer: "I'm tied up with meetings. Why don't you send over your CV?"

You: _____

_____

Employer: "We're not hiring right now."

You: _____

_____

Employer:_____ ___ _____

You: _____ _____

_____

Employer:_____

You: _____

_____

_____

6.4 BE CREATIVE

SITUATION

You've taken the conventional route in contacting employers to set up interviews. Some are receptive to speaking with you. Others are interested but not available. Then there are those you can't get through to no matter what you do. You are committed to making contact with as many employers as you can. What more can you do?

JOB SEARCH PRINCIPLE TO FOLLOW

Be creative.

Letters and CVs followed by phone calls are not the only ways to conduct a job search. Be creative in finding ways to establish contact.

Be creative as well in what you say to a potential employer or company representative when you reach her. Find some interesting ways to present the employer with a benefit that she will find difficult to refuse. Think creatively about the way you could organize your talents to fit a particular need.

STRATEGIC ACTIONS

☞ If a potential employer is nearby, stop by the office and ask for a brochure. Find out the name of the person you should see and ask the receptionist if he is in. If so, call to see if you may have a fifteen-minute interview. Don't be too pushy, however. Your dropping in unannounced may put the employer on the spot and do harm to your efforts to create a positive impression. Be ready to schedule the appointment for a later time, and leave something with the employer to pique his interest prior to the interview.

☞ Look in back issues of trade journals for the names of people who have written articles about your field. If it happens that one of them is within visiting distance, call and tell her how much you liked the article and ask if she could see you for twenty minutes to discuss your future.

☞ Find out who is on the board or key committees of associations to which you belong, and make direct contact with them.

☞ Create some power questions to pose to the potential employer on the phone to create interest in the way you think.

References

Power Speak Dorothy Leeds (Piatkus)
Cold Calling Techniques that Really Work Stephan Schiffman (Kogan Page)
Guerrilla Tactics in the New Job Market Tom Jackson (Bantam)

Turning Interviews into Offers

Mastering the interview is essential in a powerful job or career search. It is essential to know how to negotiate an opportunity within an employer's or prospective employer's domain, how to reflect the value that will excite the employer to hire you, and how to negotiate salary and benefits. The interview is the main event of your job search.

The way you prepare for an interview sets the momentum for its success. By taking the time to learn about the employer in advance, to familiarize yourself with its products and services, and to consider how your unique skills can answer the employer's needs, you will set yourself far ahead of your competition in the job search.

Prepare insightful, thoughtful questions to ask during the interview. Your questions should demonstrate your professionalism and your knowledge of the kind of work that is being proposed. They should not be questions about benefits and advancement opportunities, but about the industry and its problems and challenges. The quality of your questions can shift the employer's thinking about the job and, therefore, your possible relationship to it.

During the interview, look for every opportunity to cite an accomplishment or achievement of yours that could be translated to fulfill the employer's needs. These accomplishments do not necessarily have to be all work-related. They can be in extracurricular activities, community work, etc. Look for possibilities that could arise in the future to demonstrate that you are future-oriented and not stuck in past ways of doing things.

Keep your eyes and ears open for verbal and nonverbal feedback about how you're doing in the interview. Adjust and adapt your communication to allow the employer to discover your unique value. Be assertive, but make certain you state your value as it relates to the employer's needs, and not as a threat to him personally. Avoid statements such as: "I can turn this department around in sixty days." But say: "I know that my skill and experience will be very helpful to you in your objective to turn this department around quickly."

Your preparation includes anticipating the questions that might be asked by the employer. Look particularly for those questions that might be difficult or awkward for you to answer. Write them out in advance and practice answering them in role-play with someone else. The more you practice with both tough questions and elements of your own value assertion, the more able you will be at the actual interview.

Although you are looking for the job to fulfill your interests and targets, you will want to keep your needs in the background, particularly in the first interviews. Once the employer is interested in what you can contribute, you can start to negotiate for what you need and want.

As part of each interview you will want to negotiate your next action. Find out whom you should meet next, what additional information the employer needs, and if there is something you said that you need to revise or express more strongly to the interviewer. After the interview is over, find a quiet place to ask yourself how the interview went, what could be improved, what you've learned for future interviews, and—most importantly—what you can do to reposition yourself with the employer if you think that you made a mistake or feel that you didn't emphasize something clearly enough.

Key Job Search Principles

7.1   The interview is the main event of your job search.

7.2   Be prepared.

7.3   Ask the right questions.

7.4   Get feedback.

7.5   Translate your accomplishments to present situations.

7.6   Communicate possibilities.

7.7   Assert your magnificence.

7.8   Dress like a winner.

7.9   Look for nonverbal clues.

7.10 Anticipate questions.

7.11 Emphasize personal qualities.

7.12 Keep your needs in the background.

7.13 Close with action.

7.14 Practice with role-plays.

7.15 Repair mistakes.

7.1 THE MAIN EVENT

SITUATION

Your job search is on a roll. Your CV and cover letter communications were successful. You've reached employers on the phone, and you've racked up a number of reasonably successful interviews. You feel that you have mastered the art of self-expression in the job search. Be careful. Every interview is a major milestone with enormous possibility extending beyond it. You don't want to waste a single one.

JOB SEARCH PRINCIPLE TO FOLLOW

The interview is the main event of your job search.

Regardless of how you got there—through a perfect CV, a network contact, the recommendation of a friend, or simply by happenstance—the interview is the main event. The process of getting the job you want starts fresh with every interview. It does not matter that your CV wasn't as good as you'd like it to be, or that it took you a long or short time to get to the interview—this is it! Treat every interview as though it were exactly what you wanted. Put your full energy toward turning it into an offer.

If during the interview you decide this isn't really the job you want, don't drop your energy. Keep your enthusiasm and concentration high and see if the employer makes you an offer. In that case, you can turn the offer down, or you might find that even though you're not interested in the position under discussion, the same company has divisions and opportunities for which the interviewer could recommend you if she feels you're a viable and professional candidate.

STRATEGIC ACTIONS

☞ Gain control of the interview.

The employment interview, properly handled, is an opportunity for you to present sufficient reasons to convince the employer that you are a desirable employee. This goal is accomplished through your ability to control the interview.

Controlling the interview is a matter of attitude and confidence. The best way to feel in control is to think in advance about what you want to accomplish. Establish your agenda or objectives. In the course of the interview, ask yourself if you are meeting your objectives and tailor your answers and questions to satisfy your agenda.

A strategic agenda covers what you want to communicate about yourself, the impression you want to make, and what you want to learn about the employer. Your interview strategy should guide you to these goals:

- Making a favorable first impression and seeking common ground for communicating.
- Learning the name(s) of the person(s) you would work for.
- Discovering what the employer is looking for so that you can tailor your responses to meet his needs.
- Demonstrating that you regard yourself as an equal party in the negotiation.
- Presenting your capabilities and accomplishments in a way that suggests a solution to the employer's needs.
- Demonstrating your ability to be a contributor to the work team.
- Asking insightful questions that reveal a sincere interest in the employer and position.
- Minimizing any potential negative impressions.
- Forming an impression of the employer and surroundings; determining whether the employer and position satisfy your needs.
- Finding out who makes the hiring decision.
- Encouraging a favorable hiring decision.
- Determining the appropriate next step to take.

✍ Exercise 47: THE INTERVIEW AGENDA

Set three objectives that will help you make a strong, positive impression in the interview.

- I will _____
- I will _____
- I will _____

Set four objectives to communicate to the interviewer that you are a desirable employee who will bring value to the organization.

- I will communicate _____

_____

- I will communicate _____

_____

- I will communicate _____

_____

- I will communicate _____

_____

Set four objectives of items to find out about in the interview.

- I will find out _____
- I will find out _____
- I will find out _____
- I will find out _____

7.2 BE PREPARED

SITUATION

You can wing your way through the interview. You've done it before and got the job, so why not try it again this time?

This time is different, however. You *really* want this job. It would be a step up for you, with better pay and a chance for international travel. You know a little about the position from the printed announcement, but you don't know much about the employer. How do you go about finding that information, and how do you use it?

JOB SEARCH PRINCIPLE TO FOLLOW

Be prepared.

The interview is a demonstration to the employer of how well you get "the job" done. The job? To conduct a perfect interview. All too frequently, qualified candidates lose job opportunities because they walk into an interview unprepared and decide to "wing it." And many a corporate interviewer has lamented, "What kind of job candidate doesn't even take the initiative to find out who we are and what kind of business we do?" The way you prepare for the interview signals how you will handle the work itself.

To make the best impression on an interviewer, you want to demonstrate that you know what her company does, who its competitors are, and something about its history and personalities—especially if it's a publicly held company. Clearly, knowing about the trends in the industry itself and, to the degree possible, about particular aspects of the department or position that you're pursuing is important.

STRATEGIC ACTIONS

☞ Research the employer.

Many interviews are lost well in advance by the applicant's failure to do sufficient research to understand the employer's needs.

Good preparation offers very real advantages. It will enable you to present yourself as knowledgeable and make a better impression than other job seekers, to feel more comfortable and in control, and to better focus the interview according to your agenda. Also you will be better able to handle any problems in your background.

Direct your pre-interview research to find out:

- What products or services the employer produces or performs.

- Who the organization's customers are. What are their needs?

- How the organization's products or services are looked upon in its industry. What is their reputation?

- The organization's relationships with other businesses or agencies. Who are its major competitors?

- Recent developments or changes in the organization.

- Common industry problems.

- The most important tasks or problems that the division or department faces.

- The day-to-day tasks associated with the job.

✍ **Exercise 48: TARGET EMPLOYER NEEDS**

In the column on the left, list a task, problem, or concern that could be part of the job. Then in the space on the right, list your specific skills that relate to and can resolve the task, problem, or concern on the left. Also list accomplishments that demonstrate your ability to produce results in this area.

Employer name:_____

Key Task, Problem, or Concern	Your Related Skills, Capabilities, and Accomplishments
_____	_____
_____	_____
_____	_____
_____	_____
_____	_____
_____	_____
_____	_____
_____	_____
_____	_____
_____	_____
_____	_____
_____	_____
_____	_____

7.3 ASK GOOD QUESTIONS

SITUATION

You know that the main part of the interview will be your answering questions from the employer. Once this is done, you will be given the opportunity to ask questions of your own. You want to know more about salary and benefits, but you know that it's not appropriate to ask about those yet. How should you use your opportunity to ask questions to make a stronger impression and increase your chances for getting the job offer?

Job Search Principle to Follow

Ask the right questions.

Do not go into the interview expecting the employer to lead while you simply follow by providing the information requested. Take time in advance to consider which questions you would like answered in order to evaluate the employer's position in the marketplace, its chance of success, and what it really needs from a person in your position.

Ask questions that demonstrate the sophistication of your thinking and your ability to grapple with the problems and issues of the job. Avoid questions about salary, benefits, and other perks in the first and second interviews. Those will come later, at the time of negotiation.

List your questions in advance, take them with you on a piece of paper or in a notebook, and find the time during the interview to get clear answers to them. By demonstrating that you are precise and thoughtful you will improve the employer's estimation of you.

Strategic Actions

☞ Prepare a list of questions.

Each interview is different, and often the questions you finally ask will come to mind during the interview. Prepare your list in advance anyway. Here are some questions to consider.

- What are the most commonly faced problems in [production/advertising/distribution]?
- How would we work together on a day-to-day basis?
- How does this job fit into the overall corporate structure?
- What changes do you foresee occurring in the company during the next two years?
- How much responsibility will I have?
- What training and development would I want to undertake once I was in the position?
- What is the growth potential for the company?
- Who are the major competitors, and what are their strategies?

Use your questions as an opportunity to further highlight the value you can bring to the employer.

7.4 GET FEEDBACK

SITUATION

You're in the middle of an interview and don't know how to read the situation. You think you are responding well to the questions, but the interviewer's body language concerns you. What can you do at this point to determine if you need to change your approach?

JOB SEARCH PRINCIPLE TO FOLLOW

Get feedback.

It is all too common to go to the interview, return home, and say to yourself, "I wonder how it went." It is a good strategy to elicit feedback throughout the interviewing process. Halfway into the interview you might ask the question, "Do you believe I've got the kind of experience you're looking for?" Or, "How do you feel my experience matches up with your needs?"

Asking for a clear answer from the employer can stimulate the employer's thinking process and help you determine when you need to supply more information or improve your presentation. Don't accept it if the employer gives you an equivocal answer, e.g., "You seem to be generally qualified. We'll be interviewing other candidates . . ." Be willing to step in and ask, "Is there another person in the company you will want me to see?" Or, "What can I show you that will help you make the decision in my favor?"

STRATEGIC ACTIONS

☞ On a 3 × 5 inch index card list four questions you can ask an employer during the interview that will give you a clear reading on how you are doing, and take it with you to your next interview.

☞ If you've had interviews and were left not knowing how they worked out, think back to what questions you could have asked that would have clarified your next step. What were you avoiding by not asking those questions? List them on the 3 × 5 inch card you prepared above.

☞ After role-plays with others, ask probing questions to get accurate feedback, such as: "What could I have done to present myself better?" "How could I have improved my delivery?" "How could I have made my point more strongly?" Be sure that the people who role-play with you have the opportunity to give you honest feedback about your presentation.

$\boxed{7.5}$ Present Yourself as the Solution

Situation

You're not sure that you've got the background and experience to get the job, yet somehow you know that you *could* get the job done. You recognize that your ability is not a function of what you've learned and what you've done, but a function of your capacity to look forward and solve problems. Rather than present your employment history as history, you want to translate what you've done into a future benefit.

Job Search Principle to Follow

Translate your accomplishments to present situations.

It is not sufficient simply to rattle off the duties you've performed in past jobs and a few of your honors and awards. You need to translate past accomplishments into qualities related to what the employer wants for the future. If in response to your question the employer says, "We're looking for someone who can revitalize our direct mail marketing," a good candidate could say, "I believe that what you need is very similar to what I've done on a prior project for my last employer. For example . . ."

Speak clearly and expressively about the problems you believe you can solve and the ways you can improve or support the employer's efforts. At the same time, be careful not to threaten the person you're talking with. Don't imply that until now the job has been done poorly and that you're going to charge in and change everything. Be supportive in your approach.

Strategic Actions

☞ Offer a tangible benefit.

Employers are far more interested in what you can do for them than what you need. Ask yourself how you can help solve a problem for the employer. What can you do to provide a tangible benefit? Can you . . .

Cut costs
Use old things in new ways
Reduce waste
Make it look better
Get government support
Cut staff costs

Get it done more quickly
Turn around a bad situation
Cut downtime
Expand (virtually anything)
Preserve a competitive advantage
Provide a tax advantage

Make the boss look good
Improve packaging
Meet deadlines easily
Provide more information
Avoid potential problems
Reduce inventories
Improve the profit picture
Organize it

Improve customer support
Open more territories
Take better care of customers
Expedite the work flow
Diversify the risks
Get faster delivery
Put it on computer

✍ Exercise 49: RESULTS ORIENTATION

Identify three key problems facing the department or division you want to work in. Specify the results you can produce for the employer and how you know you can produce that result.

One result I can produce for you in this job is_____

_____

_____

The reason I know I can do this is_____

_____

_____

One result I can produce for you in this job is_____

_____

_____

The reason I know I can do this is_____

_____

_____

One result I can produce for you in this job is_____

_____

_____

The reason I know I can do this is_____

_____

_____

$\boxed{7.6}$ TALK ABOUT POSSIBILITIES

SITUATION

Most of your past jobs changed as the needs of the employer changed. Your jobs never followed a set description. In fact, the people who succeeded in the organization were the ones who actually created their own jobs by suggesting new ideas, expanding the scope of their position, and assuming new responsibilities.

Is there anything you can do in your upcoming interview to demonstrate to the employer that you offer far more than she expects?

JOB SEARCH PRINCIPLE TO FOLLOW

Communicate possibilities.

Remember that an employer frequently will be interviewing to fill a job description that might have been created several years ago. The job description may not adequately represent the potential of the position, only what has been done to date.

Use your imagination to expand the employer's thinking about the position into future opportunities, goals, and potential. Use power questions to stimulate the employer's vision of what can happen with somebody competent and imaginative (like you) on the job.

STRATEGIC ACTIONS

✍ Exercise 50: EXPANDING THE JOB

As part of your preparation for the interview, find out everything you can about the job and the employer's needs as they are now. Then create an expanded vision of the job. Answer the following questions to guide you toward this vision.

In an expanded view of the job, how could it be done more efficiently and at a lower cost?

_____

_____

In an expanded view of the job, what innovative ideas could be considered?

_____

_____

In an expanded view of the job, what could be done to make the work environment more vibrant and exciting?

_____

_____

In an expanded view of the job, what could be done to help others attain maximum performance and increased personal satisfaction?

_____

_____

In an expanded view of the job, what could be done to improve the product or service that the organization provides?

_____

_____

In an expanded view of the job, what could be done to make customers or clients more satisfied with the product or service?

_____

_____

In an expanded view of the job, what else would improve or change?

_____

_____

_____

_____

_____

_____

[7.7] ASSERT YOUR MAGNIFICENCE

SITUATION

It's hard to know how to present yourself in an interview. It's easy to speak about your limitations, failings, and problems, but talking about your skills, abilities, qualities, accomplishments, and other attributes feels like boasting or bragging. As you approach interviews, you are afraid you might unconsciously fall back to a bland self-presentation.

JOB SEARCH PRINCIPLE TO FOLLOW

Assert your magnificence.

Don't be afraid to speak well of yourself at the interview. Assert your assets, especially your willingness to take on challenges and to do whatever it takes to create results. The qualities of willingness and energy often produce more success in an interview than the specifics of your accomplishments. Willpower and sureness of self-expression count highly in interviews for jobs that are changing. Frequently what you have already learned will not be sufficient for a job or industry that is rapidly evolving, whereas your ability to learn quickly and master complex changes could make you the best candidate.

STRATEGIC ACTIONS

☞ Demonstrate a positive energy level.

One of the greatest qualities you can convey at an interview is a strong helping of positive energy. Positive energy is equated with motivation, which can be a major factor in a favorable evaluation. Some energy reminders:

- Greet the interviewer with focused attention and interest.
- Shake hands firmly, but don't crush any bones.
- Be alert, establish eye contact, and project certainty and optimism.
- Listen actively and respond with certainty.
- Keep your posture upright and, at the same time, relaxed.
- Avoid physical signs of nervousness—tapping your fingers, moving around in your seat. (If you *are* nervous, admit it without apology.)
- Keep your communications to the point; don't wander off the subject very far.
- When seated, don't close yourself off by crossing your arms and legs.

7.8 DRESS LIKE A WINNER

SITUATION

As you prepare to go to an interview, look in the mirror and ask yourself: "What do I wear? How do I decide?"

JOB SEARCH PRINCIPLE TO FOLLOW

Dress like a winner.

The way you present yourself—your clothes, posture, and grooming—communicates a great deal. Pay attention to how you look and provide yourself with the clothes and grooming appropriate to a successful person. Notice how successful people in your field dress, and use that as your guide.

Ask others to give you feedback about how you look and how to improve your presentation. Even if you're going into a field in which informality is standard, dress somewhat more formally for the interview. The way people work may call for one style of dress, and the way they present themselves to others in meetings and interviews may call for another.

STRATEGIC ACTIONS

☞ Enhance your personal appearance.

Most people dress out of habit and often lose sight of how they come across to others. Dress in a way that supports your purpose in life, not simply in the way that is familiar to you.

- Even if you are on a tight budget, dress in a way that communicates success—it is better to have fewer well-fitting clothes of good quality than more clothes of lower quality.
- Make sure that what you wear is clean and well pressed.
- Dress on the conservative side, with an accent or accessory that gives you an extra bit of spark.
- Women seeking professional positions should dress in conservative suits or well-made skirts and blouses. Avoid clanking jewelry, heavy fragrances, or too much makeup.
- Men seeking professional positions should invest in at least one high-quality business suit. Show up well shaved, with shined shoes, clean nails, and a recent haircut. Pinky rings, gold chains, and loud braces should be left at home.

7.9 UNDERSTANDING NONVERBAL CLUES

SITUATION

You seem to be missing something. You've had several interviews and not a single callback or offer. Reviewing past interviews, you're not really certain how you did or how you came across. You start to worry that perhaps you're not getting the right feedback.

JOB SEARCH PRINCIPLE TO FOLLOW

Look for nonverbal clues.

Keep your ears and eyes open. If the interviewer appears inattentive or distracted, bring the interview back on track by changing the subject or asking a question. Check with the interviewer from time to time to see if you're providing enough information. Ask: "Would you like to hear more about this?" Notice when the interviewer is taking notes and use this to determine what seems to be important to her.

STRATEGIC ACTIONS:

☞ Tune into body language.

Learning to recognize both verbal and nonverbal messages and to communicate intentionally with your body language allows you better to interpret what is happening in the interview and to take the strategic actions needed to make the best impression.
   Review the following body language scenarios.

What you communicate:

Mastery.   You arrive five minutes before the interview and stop in the bathroom to adjust your thinking and review your aims. Your clothes fit. On meeting the interviewer, you give a firm handshake. Seated for the interview, you are attentive and relaxed, your voice tone varying from excited (energetic) to pensive (the short silence of contemplation before answering a tough question). You take notes and ask for clarification when needed. You don't apologize. You are aware of the interviewer's movements, and at signals of wandering or inattention you shift your approach, change your tone of voice, and ask a question.

Insecurity.   You arrive a half hour before the interview. Your clothes are a bit rumpled and your outfit is all plain vanilla, without a touch of class. You give a rather distracted handshake, wring your hands, and tug at your collar. In the interview you sink into the "hot seat," crossing both arms and legs. You try to make eye contact, but find a spot on the floor that your eyes seem magnetized to.

When the questioning begins you clear your throat before answering and are so busy wondering how the interview is going that you hear only part of what the interviewer just said. Rather than admit you missed it, you guess.

What you see:

Interest.   The interviewer concentrates on your answers and takes notes from time to time. When you are answering there is a slight lean forward, and a small nod indicates that you are on track. When you smile you see it reciprocated as the interviewer mirrors your presentation slightly.

Inattention.   The interviewer keeps you waiting and takes a phone call during the interview. You get the sense that when you are responding to a question that the interviewer asked, he is thinking of the next question and not listening to your answers. Noticing these danger signals, you ask for feedback—"Do you think I have the qualifications you are looking for?"—or politely ask the interviewer to clarify something he said before, not putting him on the spot, but waking him to his job.

☞   Improve your listening skills.

An important aspect of nonverbal communication is your ability to listen clearly and understand not only the words being said but also their implications and underlying context. See if you can pick up patterns in the questions asked. Is the interviewer focusing heavily on organizational skills or personal relationships? Is she asking significant questions, or has she perhaps already made a decision and is just filling the time?

When you're asked a question, don't rush in with your answer before the last words are out of the interviewer's mouth. Pause for a few seconds, relax, frame your response, and then reply. Silence can communicate control, and even a three-second pause will create the impression that you are relaxed and confident.

7.10 WHY SHOULD I HIRE YOU?

SITUATION

You've had a few problems with your interviews. You notice that you often get distracted by questions you weren't prepared to answer.

JOB SEARCH PRINCIPLE TO FOLLOW

Anticipate questions.

Put yourself in the place of the employer and ask yourself, "What would I need to know in order to make a hiring decision?" Anticipate questions related to experience, familiarity with the organization, education, training, and accomplishments that would best prepare you for the job.

STRATEGIC ACTIONS

✍ Exercise 51: TOUGH QUESTIONS

If you are aware of the employer's objectives in asking a question you will be better prepared to give the strongest answers. Review the following questions that arise in most interviews and write down the main points you would want to make in response to each.

Why did you leave your last job?

Employer's objective: to determine your career direction and level of ambition; to identify any problems related to your career change.

Your objective: to communicate that getting this job is part of your plan to improve yourself and advance your career.

Points you want to make:_____

_____

_____

What were your duties and responsibilities?

Employer's objective: to measure your accomplishments against your responsibilities. Did you produce adequate results or could you have achieved more?

Your objective: to directly relate past accomplishments, duties, and responsibilities to the employer's present needs.

Points you want to make: _____

_____

_____

What were the most difficult challenges of your most recent job?

Employer's objective: to compare the pressure of your past job to the pressure you would face on the job he wants to fill.
Your objective: to assure the employer that you can work under pressure.

Points you want to make: _____
_____
_____

(To a new graduate) What were your extracurricular activities?

Employer's objective: to determine the range of your interests and activities. How versatile an employee will you be? Will you take on additional projects if necessary?
Your objective: to describe extracurricular activities so that your ability to contribute is clear.

Points you want to make: _____
_____
_____

(To a new graduate) What were your most enjoyable subjects? What subjects did you do best in?

Employer's objective: to determine the relevance of your education and major. Did you perform consistently better in your major courses than in required courses?
Your objective: to highlight aspects of your education that best reveal solid accomplishments.

Points you want to make: _____
_____
_____

What was your relationship to your previous boss?

Employer's objective: to identify any potential problems in your way of relating to others and taking supervision.
Your objective: to communicate that you work well on a team.

Points you want to make:_____
_____
_____

How many people reported to you? How would you describe your management style?

Employer's objective: to evaluate your ability to work with and manage others.

Your objective: to highlight your most significant accomplishments in managing others in a way that relates to the present employer's needs.

Points you want to make:_____

_____

_____

What kind of training courses have you taken? What have you learned on your job?

Employer's objective: to determine the potential value of your training; to measure your interest in developing your capability on the job.

Your objective: to communicate a strong motivation to develop and grow in job performance.

Points you want to make:_____

_____

_____

What were the bottom-line results that your job contributed to the organization?

Employer's objective: to determine your ability to produce results and your awareness and concern for the bottom line.

Your objective: to communicate the value you have created for others.

Points you want to make:_____

_____

_____

☞ Other questions:

Listed below are questions frequently asked in interviews. Prepare your answers as you did above. First, determine the employer's reason for asking the question. Then ask yourself what you can say that communicates your ability to do the job and produce positive results for the employer.

Questions about your personality and ability to communicate

• Tell me about yourself.

• What motivates you in your work?

- What interests you in our company?
- What kind of personal growth do you seek?
- What unique qualities do you see yourself bringing to this group?
- What are your greatest strengths? Greatest weaknesses?
- How do you perform under pressure?
- What type of people do you prefer to work with?

Questions about your education, training, and skills

- What did you learn in school or college that will help you in this job?
- How did your academic experience prepare you for your career?
- Describe the accomplishments in school or college of which you are most proud.
- How difficult was school or college for you?
- Why did you choose this field?

Questions about your work history and experience

- What in your past work experience particularly relates to our needs?
- What is the worst/best thing your previous employer could say about you?
- How quickly could you make a contribution to our organization?
- Describe your relationship with your former supervisors.
- Why did you leave your last job?
- What were your greatest accomplishments in your last job?
- What difficulties did you have in your last position?
- What aspects of your performance do you think could be most improved?
- Give an example of a problem you encountered in your previous job, and tell how you handled it.

Questions about your goals and reasons for wanting the job

- What are your long-term career goals? How will this job help you meet them?
- Where do you want to be five years from now?
- How long will you stay with the job if we offer it to you?

☞ Know how to answer the biggest question of all:

Why should I hire you?

This is the fundamental, underlying question. Keep it in front of you at all times, in every conversation you have with a potential employer. By keeping in mind what you can do to anticipate and meet an employer's needs, you will be well on the way to maximizing your effectiveness in the interview.

7.11 EXPRESS YOUR QUALITIES

SITUATION

You've determined that your education and past experience do not relate directly to your current career target. You know you can do the work, but how do you express this?

JOB SEARCH PRINCIPLE TO FOLLOW

Emphasize personal qualities.

Traditional job marketing stresses skills, education, and experience. Although these are important, skills and education can quickly become obsolete, and experience is less relevant because of the fast changes in technology and the marketplace. Stress the qualities of your character and your work, your innovation, trustworthiness, integrity, and so on. Qualitative attributes can substitute for experience. Always stress the primary qualities of willingness, motivation, and enthusiasm.

STRATEGIC ACTIONS

✍ **Exercise 52: PERSONAL QUALITIES DEMO**

Cite a past situation or accomplishment that demonstrates each of the qualities below.

Accurate   _____

Ambitious   _____

Confident   _____

Cooperative   _____

Dependable   _____

Detail-oriented   _____

Energetic   _____

Fast   _____

Highly motivated   _____

Imaginative   _____

Managerial   _____

Personable   _____

Productive   _____

Quality-oriented   _____

Quick-thinking   _____

Reliable   _____

Responsible   _____

Risk-taking   _____

Self-assured   _____

Smart   _____

Versatile   _____

Willing   _____

List other qualities:

_____   _____

_____   _____

_____   _____

_____   _____

_____   _____

7.12 Take the Spotlight Off Your Needs

Situation

The neediest people get the worst jobs. On the other hand, without a job, running out of resources, and with no offers on the table, you need a definite boost in self-esteem. The little voice in the back of your head wants you to throw yourself down in front of the employer's desk and plead for "something—just something!" Don't.

Job Search Principle to Follow

Keep your needs in the background.

Searching for a job is often very trying. Particularly if you are unemployed, there may be so many hopes riding on an interview that a certain desperation can take over and kill your chances. Keep your needs in the background, and don't act as though your life depended on the results of this interview.

Avoid questions about salary, benefits, etc., in the first one or two interviews with the same company.

If you can, try to give the employer the impression that there are many opportunities before you and this is only one of them.

Strategic Actions

☞ Find someone in your extended family or a counselor or therapist to whom you can communicate your personal fears and needs. By acknowledging fears openly to the right person you can separate them from the impression you need to make in your interview.

7.13 Close with Action

Situation

The tendency in an interview is to keep the relationship with the potential employer friendly and comfortable. Sometimes you can keep it *so* comfortable that you forget to ask those tough questions about what to do next. You may shy away from putting the employer on the spot from an innate politeness and fail to advance the action to the next phase.

Job Search Principle to Follow

Close with action.

Don't leave the interview empty-handed. Do whatever you can to assure that the employer will take the next step. At the least, determine what the next step is.

Take a few moments to summarize the interview and then ask, "What is the next step to bring us closer to a decision?" Perhaps the employer will say, "Well, we plan to interview a number of candidates, and we will evaluate the results and make our decision." This is not really satisfactory. Follow up with another question to try to pin down the employer:

"Is there any way I can help you expedite the process?"

"Is there someone else whom I should see in the organization?"

"What else do you need to know about me to make a decision?"

"What is your timing?"

Don't be afraid to go the extra mile with the right closing questions. When the interview ends on vague terms it leaves you in a sense of suspended animation and could result in disappointment. Remember to ask your questions without sounding desperate.

STRATEGIC ACTIONS

✍ Exercise 53: CLOSING STATEMENT

In advance of your next interview, complete the following statement, which summarizes why you should get an offer.

There are three reasons I should work in your organization: First, I bring the skills, abilities, and qualities that will make me a successful _____; second, I will produce results for this organization and work at maximum performance levels; and third, this opportunity is aligned with my career goals and will give me the chance to expand and grow. Let me explain further:

*Regarding my capabilities, I*_____

_____

_____

_____

*Regarding my ability to produce results and contribute to the success of this organization, I*_____

_____

_____

_____

*Finally, regarding my career goals, I see this as an ideal opportunity to*_____

_____

_____

_____

Close with a powerful question:

What is the next step to bring us closer to a decision?
(or)_____

_____

_____

7.14 PRACTICE

SITUATION

No one ever taught you how to interview. The only interviews you've had are for *real jobs,* so you haven't had time to experiment. Don't let the success of your future depend on trying to find out how to interview "on the job." Take time to practice. The better the rehearsal—the better the performance.

JOB SEARCH PRINCIPLE TO FOLLOW
Practice with role-plays.

Sitting across from an employer's desk is *not* the time to practice. Even though it may seem a little awkward or embarrassing, it is useful to get two or three people together in role-play interviews.

Try to set up your role-plays with people who resemble the type of person you are likely to have interviews with. It is generally not as realistic to use a spouse or relative for this.

STRATEGIC ACTIONS

☞ Plan a role-play.

Find a career counselor or someone with a background not too far off your job target who is willing to take an hour to role-play with you.

Prepare six or eight questions you might be asked in the interview, including some tough ones.

Brief the person playing the employer on the kind of job you're looking for and what the interviewer might be looking for or concerned about. Have this person read your CV and the questions you've suggested, and give him a few minutes to prepare.

If you can, tape-record the role-plays to review later. Ask the person playing the employer to take a few notes along the way as a real employer would.

Enter the room and greet the "employer" as you would in a real-life situation. Then allow the "employer" to conduct an interview as authentically as possible. Don't comment on the questions while the interview is going on.

If possible, invite a third person as an observer. The third party should watch the entire interaction—your body language, listening skills, and energy level—since the person playing the employer may be too caught up in his role.

After fifteen minutes, stop the interview and ask the "employer" and the observer to comment on what worked and what didn't work about the interview. Ask: "What could have been improved in the way I presented myself?"

Listen to the feedback and make notes. Don't defend, explain, or justify, as this could shut down the person's willingness to give you accurate feedback. Probe with questions that elicit detail, such as: "Could I have been more assertive?" "Did I relate well enough to your needs?" "Do you think I listened closely enough?"

You should practice the role-play two or three times with variations. When you come up against unanticipated tough questions you can set those aside and use them in mini–role-plays later.

7.15 | REPAIR MISTAKES

SITUATION

You goofed. You blew it. You don't really know what you were thinking of, but you forgot a major slice of information that would have made that last employer much more interested in you. It's time for damage control.

JOB SEARCH PRINCIPLE TO FOLLOW

Repair mistakes.

It is all too common to criticize yourself after an interview for questions you forgot to ask or answers that were not fully formed nor as powerful as they could be. Rather than criticize yourself, you should take action toward repairing mistakes and strengthening responses that were weak or incomplete.

If you feel that you totally blew it you should request a second interview.

It is a positive trait to want to correct what you consider to be mistakes or weaknesses, not just hope that the employer didn't notice. It demonstrates that you are the kind of employee who would take the same positive action in response to the mistakes that inevitably occur on the job itself.

STRATEGIC ACTIONS

☞ Compose a letter addressed to the employer with the purpose of conveying or clarifying those ideas you neglected to state or didn't state clearly enough in the interview.

Tell the employer that you think you performed poorly in the interview and that you'd like to meet again.

References

The First Five Minutes Norman King (Simon and Schuster)
Great Answers to Tough Interview Questions Martin John Yate (Kogan Page)
How to Talk so People Listen Sonya Hamlin (Thorsons)
How to Win at Interviews Iain Maitland (Century)
How to Turn an Interview into a Job Jeffrey Allen (Simon & Schuster, audio cassette)
Sweaty Palms: The Neglected Art of Being Interviewed Anthony Medley (Ten Speed Press)

Strategic Follow-up

Whenever you achieve an advance in your job search campaign, the next move is to protect and secure it. After an interview, you want to secure the ground you've gained and even add to it. This is the purpose of strategic follow-up—to strengthen the employer's interest and her recognition that you are the person to hire.

A thank-you letter is not a follow-up strategy. It is a necessary nicety that usually gets overlooked or discarded.

Immediately after every interview it is essential that you consider how the interview went and what aspects of your presentation need to be improved, underlined, or strengthened. List those areas you still have questions about, as well as the information you would have liked to have obtained from the interview but missed or need clarified.

Follow up quickly, especially if you have questions to ask. A call within twenty-four hours of the interview will usually get fast recognition. If you wait too long the likelihood of response dims.

A speedy follow-up will create momentum. Ask your questions and let the employer know that you'll be staying in touch. Keep the momentum by finding out what the next stages of the hiring process are, i.e., who the next people to see are, what the criteria are that determine if you will get an offer, or how long it will take to make the decision.

If you've made several attempts to follow up, including telephone calls and letters, and you still don't hear anything, don't keep writing. Consider the situation dead and transfer your attention to the next interview. This doesn't mean to throw away your records. You may want to conduct another follow-up in thirty to sixty days. The main thing is not to entertain more hope and invest more energy than is warranted.

If, on the other hand, your dialogue with the employer continues and you gain new insight into the job, do not hesitate to ask for a second or third meeting—with the person whom you've already met or with someone else in the hiring chain. Don't wait to be asked. You can initiate the request.

Key Job Search Principles

8.1   Debrief after each interview.

8.2   A thank-you letter is not a follow-up strategy.

8.3   When in doubt, find out.

8.4   Don't wait in line.

8.5   Recalibrate your presentation.

8.1 DEBRIEF THOROUGHLY

SITUATION

Given what it has taken to arrange an interview, prepare for it, and take it, there can be a tendency, after it's over, to sit back, breathe a sigh of relief, and wait. Don't do this. As soon after the interview as possible, find a time to fully debrief yourself about what happened and make notes about what needs to be done next.

JOB SEARCH PRINCIPLE TO FOLLOW

Debrief after each interview.

Keep accurate notes about all your interviews and conversations with potential employers. Otherwise, when your job search gets busy you could find that important details about past meetings will elude you. Record all the actions you've taken and what further follow-up is required.

STRATEGIC ACTIONS

✍ Exercise 54: INTERVIEW DEBRIEF

Immediately following each interview, while it is fresh in your mind, evaluate your performance, summarize what you learned about the employer, and determine the next steps to take. Answer the following questions:

Name of organization:_____

Person(s) interviewed:_____Date:_____

Describe the rapport between you and the interviewer._____

_____

_____

_____

_____

What was the best part of your presentation (that you may want to re-inforce)?_____

What information did you lack about the company?_____

_____

_____

_____

What information about yourself did you *not* convey clearly (that you want to present again)?_____

_____

_____

_____

What could have been improved?_____

_____

_____

_____

What are the most *positive* impressions you gave the employer?_____

_____

_____

_____

_____

What are the most *negative* impressions you gave the employer?_____

_____

_____

_____

_____

If you got the job, what would be your strongest contribution?_____

_____

_____

_____

What questions do you still need answers to?_____

_____

_____

_____

What information about your ability to produce results should you reinforce
with the employer?_____

_____

_____

What information about yourself would you like to add?_____

_____

_____

What will it take to get an offer from this employer?_____

_____

_____

What else needs to be noted from this interview?_____

_____

_____

Other questions:_____

_____

_____

_____

Summary of follow-up actions to take
Based on your answers above, what actions do you need to take *now* to accelerate an offer from this employer?

_____

_____

_____

_____

_____

_____

8.2 DON'T RELY ON THANK-YOU LETTERS

SITUATION

You've had a few interviews, and now you prepare to send out a few polite thank-you letters. It's time to reappraise this traditional approach.

JOB SEARCH PRINCIPLE TO FOLLOW

A thank-you letter is not a follow-up strategy.

After the interview it is important to convey the right message to the employer. The right message is not simply a thank-you, but a follow-up that will position you in light of what you now know about the employer and what you have that he needs. In your follow-up letter reinforce those points you felt to be well accepted by the employer, adding whatever information you may have gathered after the interview that will communicate your understanding of the job. Clarify and strengthen whatever ideas or qualities you feel you may not have communicated well, and raise whatever questions occurred to you after the interview.

The follow-up letter is a means to advance the action toward a job offer, not just a gesture of good manners.

STRATEGIC ACTIONS

✍ Exercise 55: YOUR FOLLOW-UP STRATEGY

In your follow-up—whether by phone, in person, or by fax or mail—you want to accelerate the decision-making process by stressing the benefits you can offer the employer. Using the information in Exercise 54, complete the following sentences:

Opening: Thank the employer.

I want to thank you for the opportunity to discuss_____

_____

_____

_____

Repeat the benefit you offer.

After reviewing our discussion, I know that I can make a successful contribution to your organization by_____

_____

_____

_____

Provide additional information.

In addition to what we discussed, I would like you to know_____

_____

_____

_____

Clear up any misconceptions or confusion (if necessary).

_____

_____

_____

_____

☞ Suggestion for composing the follow-up letter:

- Address the letter to the interviewer by name. If you do not know the correct spelling and title, call and get them.

- If you were interviewed by several different people in the organization on the same visit, send the letter to the principle interviewer or hiring authority. Send copies of this with an individualized cover note to the other people who interviewed you.

- The letter should be neatly printed on letterhead stationery.

- Mail, fax, or hand deliver the letter within twenty-four hours of the interview. A timely communication will set you apart from your competition.

8.3 ASK QUESTIONS

SITUATION

Most interviews are imperfect. You didn't take detailed notes since you were concentrating on the interviewer, and now you've discovered that there are some things you've either missed or didn't hear. It's time to take stock.

JOB SEARCH PRINCIPLE TO FOLLOW

When in doubt, find out.

After the interview, make a short list of what you know and what you don't know about where you stand with the employer. Call the employer within a day or two, while the relationship is still current, and get answers to those questions.

STRATEGIC ACTION

Review the list of questions below, and determine if you have clear answers. Decide what additional information you still need to know, then get on the phone with the person with whom you interviewed, and get the additional information:

- What is the next step the employer is going to take?
- What's the next step you should take to be sure the employer knows everything he needs to know to make a decision?
- What's the target decision date on this job?
- Who are the customers of this organization?
- What are the competitive factors facing the work group or organization?
- What qualities about yourself do you have to reinforce in the mind of the employer?

8.4 ACCELERATING ACTION-MEETING OBJECTIONS

SITUATION

Your job search has been drawn out and inconclusive. You feel as if the whole thing is stuck in molasses and you have to drag yourself through it.

It's time to spark some initiative, create some action, and hurdle all the barriers that block your way to getting job offers.

JOB SEARCH PRINCIPLE TO FOLLOW

Don't wait in line.

The job search can be lengthy. If the employer procrastinates or is indecisive it can get painfully drawn out. Once you and the employer clarify the next steps, politely hold him to the plan. Obviously, you can't railroad him, but you *can* call him to ask how the process is moving along and if there is a new target date that he wants to set or something else that you can do to expedite a decision.

Resistance by the employer can come in many forms, from needing more time to make a decision to specific concerns regarding your candidacy. Acknowledge that you understand the problem *and* that you still want to move the process along in a timely way.

STRATEGIC ACTIONS

✍ Exercise 56: MEETING OBJECTIONS

In recontacting employers, you will rarely elicit a definite answer on your first attempt. You will most likely run into a variety of obstacles: The employer may not have made a decision yet and is stalling for more time. Or she may have legitimate concerns about your qualifications or ability to do the job. In either case, make sure you handle the objection by: (1) acknowledging the employer's concern (don't argue or tell her she is wrong); (2) responding to the concern with a benefit that you can offer; (3) restating your interest in the job; and (4) pushing for a decision.

The following are objections and obstacles that you may encounter as you follow up with employers. Write your responses to them.

You just don't have the right education for the job.

Your response: _____

_____

We've narrowed the candidates down to three and will probably choose one of these.

Your response: _____

_____

We have too many good applicants to choose from and have not made a decision yet.

Your response: _____

_____

We don't feel that you can do the job.

Your response: _____

_____

We're looking for someone more experienced.

Your response: _____

_____

We've decided to postpone hiring someone at this time.

Your response: _____

_____

☞ When the opportunity looks dim, drop it.

Don't delude yourself into thinking that there's an offer on the way when there isn't. If you have followed up with the employer over a four-to-eight-week period and he is not returning your phone calls, or you're sensing that there may be a long delay in hiring, don't keep this possibility on your "hope" list. Then if something positive does happen, it will be a gift. Keep paring your active list so that you are looking at real opportunities and are not stuck in wishful holding patterns.

8.5 UPGRADE YOUR PRESENTATION

SITUATION

You are on a trail of disappointment. The employment situation isn't getting any better, and, most importantly, your hard-won interviews are not panning out. You have rehearsed your approach and think it works well but are getting no responses from the employers you have met with. The little voice in the back of your head tells you it's time to resign yourself to the idea of cutting back your expectations. Before you quit . . .

JOB SEARCH PRINCIPLE TO FOLLOW

Recalibrate your presentation.

Use every interview as an opportunity to reexamine how you are presenting yourself, what your CV looks like, etc. As you debrief, make some notes on what someone else might say about your presentation. Were you late, did you let the employer do all the talking, etc.? What can you improve in your presentation next time?

In giving yourself accurate feedback and then practicing the necessary adjustments in your role-plays, you will create for yourself a successful presentation. If you're not sure why things aren't working, it's best to engage a good coach or counselor, or someone who will be able to help you pinpoint your weak points. Then you can practice improvements in further role-plays. It's this constant recalibration and improvement that will lead to ultimate success and victory in your job search.

Strategic Actions

✍ Exercise 57: PRESENTATION UPGRADE

Use the following form to find ways to enhance your performance at interviews. Make a note of anything you can think of that you might improve. Get feedback on these ideas from someone in your personal network.

A way to improve my preparation for the interview:_____

_____

_____

A way to improve my advance understanding of the employer's needs:____

_____

_____

A way to improve my personal appearance/presentation:_____

_____

_____

A way to improve interviewer's perception of the value I offer:_____

_____

_____

A way to improve my responses to the employer's questions:_____

_____

_____

A way to improve my poise and self-confidence:_____

_____

_____

_____

A way to improve my handling of my weak points:_____

_____

_____

_____

A way to improve my ability to rebound from mistakes:_____

_____

_____

_____

A way to improve my ability to close the interview with a proposal for action:_____

_____

_____

Closing the Deal and Negotiating Compensation

*I*n the closing stages of your strategic job search you will address the material *and* psychological rewards that come with your new position. The way you negotiate your terms of employment will have an important impact on short- and long-term earnings and personal rewards. We believe that career satisfaction and good earnings are both essential. The work itself produces the satisfaction, and the salary pays the bills.

Material success does not always translate into personal satisfaction and fulfillment. It is, however, an attractive lure. Many people chase ever-increasing job responsibilities and upward mobility, hoping to gain what they call success. Frequently they end up disappointed. We don't object to the quest for success. Our preference is for you to create a blend of material satisfaction and enhancement of personal values. We believe that the people who have the most passion for their work ultimately earn in the upper brackets of their field.

The formula for making money is a simple one: *Money follows value*. If you're not making the money you deserve, the first step is to look at how to increase your value in the job. If you're being offered a new position and the salary isn't what you'd like it to be, you should stress to the employer that your work will generate positive value for the organization. It is the value you add that generates the funds to pay you.

Because money is such a sensitive issue for many of us, it's wise to do research in advance about what's being paid for different jobs. Once you've been offered the position, your tendency may be to leave the salary up to the employer. People frequently feel that they can't negotiate salary, but must either accept or reject what's offered. By learning about what salaries are being paid in your field and in the location in which you're negotiating, you develop a basis for negotiation.

At the beginning of salary negotiations you want to find out what the employer has in mind before stating your own objectives. If your salary needs are on the table first, the employer can accept the figure if it's lower than his intended offer or negotiate it down if it's higher. When a salary range is verbalized, go for the top figure. Don't undercut yourself by thinking that in accepting the lower figure you make yourself more attractive to the employer. If an employer is truly interested in you, you will find a surprising degree of willingness to negotiate upward.

Prepare yourself for negotiation. In your sweaty-palmed desire to tie things up and resolve your job search anxieties, don't cave in to the employer's ideas of what your compensation should be. Be sure to include your personal work-style needs in the negotiation. These could include your work schedule, time off, ability to work at home, travel considerations, and ongoing training.

The final word: *Be outrageous.* Don't let any defiencies in your past salary levels impede you from achieving the salary range you feel is warranted by what you can now contribute. Dispel any image you have of yourself as earning below scale due to your history or supposed educational shortcomings. Negotiate from the position that you will operate at 100% of your potential. Go for what you're worth, and know that what you're worth is a function of your commitment to deliver great value.

Key Job Search Principles

9.1 Make more money.

9.2 Money follows value.

9.3 Research pays off.

9.4 Negotiate!

9.5 Don't cave in.

9.6 Work style is negotiable.

9.7 Break out of salary traps.

9.1 MAKE MORE MONEY

SITUATION

It's been a long haul from job targeting to negotiating the offer. You're proud of your movement and success, and you probably feel a little bit humbled by the effort it took. You may have discovered that the expertise you thought was easily marketable was not, and that it took a lot of persistent work to achieve a job offer. As you move to the negotiating table for final discussions, you may feel tempted to get the negotiation over with and get on the payroll fast. Don't. The cost to your next decade of earning power could be enormous. Go for a full and assertive salary negotiation that brings you as close as possible to the top of the current salary range in the job you'll be accepting.

JOB SEARCH PRINCIPLE TO FOLLOW

Make more money.

Keep your earning power high. Use every opportunity to increase the money that you're making. This is not as obvious as it sounds. First of all, making more money doesn't necessarily ensure greater satisfaction in life. The satisfaction in your life comes from your relationship to what you do; your self-expression at work. On the other hand, by increasing your earning power, you will be given jobs of greater scope and challenge, and, assuming they are in your field of choice, ones that are more satisfying. Working at a higher salary, you will be given greater support tools, greater range, and probably greater freedom. In every negotiation keep pushing for the extra increments that will bring you to the top of your job's salary range. Then perform in a way that justifies what you are being paid. A thousand-pound difference in salary early in your career, with compound interest and salary increases based on that advantage, could end up being worth a hundred times that by the end of your career.

STRATEGIC ACTIONS

☞ Get a mental picture of yourself in the new job: See how you work, your style, your relationship with customers and colleagues. Then imagine someone at a more senior level in that same job and see how she handles it: whom she'd be meeting with, talking to, negotiating with, etc. Now overlay one view on the other, and see if you can visualize what you could be doing in a much bigger way than you have up till now. For example, if you've been the sales manager for a £25-million company, see what would be different if you were the sales manager for a £75-million company in the same product line. How would you be working in a bigger and more exciting way?

☞ Think of someone you consider highly successful in his field—a person you've met or observed in action. What is there about his presentation or approach that garners high respect and responsibility? Identify how you could improve your presentation.

✍ Exercise 58: JOB OFFER EVALUATION

Evaluate each job offer in terms of the tangible (salary) and intangible (satisfaction factors) values that it creates for you by completing the following checklist. Translate nonpay benefits into pounds in terms of equivalent value (i.e., what amount would you be willing to subtract from the paycheck of a high-paying job that didn't offer this?). This is not meant to be an accounting exercise, just a way to strengthen your sense of the value of your job offers.

Reward Factor	Monetary Value, or What It Might Be Worth to You (Estimate)
Starting salary offered	_____
Probable salary in three years	_____
Bonus opportunities	_____
Benefits:	
Health insurance	_____
Other insurance	_____
Vacation	_____
Maternity/paternity leave	_____
Retirement/pension benefits	_____
Other	_____
Hidden savings (e.g., shorter commuting distance, dress code)	_____
How the job fits in with future career plans	_____
Training and educational opportunities	_____
Potential for advancement	_____
Quality of work environment	_____
Job security	_____
Opportunity to adjust job requirements for family obligations and personal pursuits	_____
Morale in the organization	_____
Other considerations	_____
_____	_____
_____	_____
_____	_____
_____	_____

9.2 MONEY FOLLOWS VALUE

SITUATION

The thought continues to haunt you even now as you approach the salary negotiation: "I need a job," "The economy is rotten," "It's hard to get a job at all, let alone a decent, well-paying one." Notice how fears of scarcity and difficulty can tinge a job campaign, especially in a tough economy. You want to make sure that you don't blow it. A part of you says, "Don't mess around with this one, you need the job, you need a stable income, take what they offer you." Our recommendation: Don't settle too easily.

JOB SEARCH PRINCIPLE TO FOLLOW

Money follows value.

The way to earn more money is to produce more value. Once you produce more value, if you haven't significantly increased your income, the only thing left to do is to produce more value still. As you continue to produce more value, ultimately the restraints will break and money will roll in. This is universally true, although of course there are many barriers and blocks that are difficult to surmount.

STRATEGIC ACTIONS

✍ Exercise 59: VALUE ADDED

Take time to develop a list of all the things you can do to create value for a future employer, not only in the normal tasks of the job, but in relationships, cost savings, innovation, creativity, and ideas of new ways to expand the enterprise. As hard as it may seem, try to put pound figures to these benefits so that in your negotiation you will be in a good position to talk about the value that you can produce. Make your best guess.

Value You Can Create	Cost Savings/Increased Revenues
By building new relationships I can:	£ Value
_____	_____
_____	_____
_____	_____
By spending smartly I can:	£ Value
_____	_____
_____	_____
_____	_____

By generating new revenues I can: £ Value

_____ _____   _____

_____   _____

_____   _____

By stimulating innovation and   £ Value
creativity I can:

_____   _____

_____   _____

_____   _____

By finding new markets I can: £ Value

_____   _____

_____   _____

_____   _____

In other areas I can: £ Value

_____   _____

_____   _____

_____   _____

☞   Pick a salary figure that is worth reaching for and that makes you feel successful. Now set up a role-play with a tape recorder, a friend, or preferably both. Pose the question: "Why should I hire you?" Answer it. Pose another question: "Why are you valuable to us?" Answer that. Now pose a third question: "What can you do for me that's worth more than £_____ [double your salary target]?" Answer that. Keep practicing with these questions until you can comfortably communicate, without hesitation, how you're worth the money you want to make.

9.3 RESEARCH PAYS OFF

SITUATION

It feels good to have the job offer in hand. You relax and let your guard down, knowing that you've come a long way and that this final stage should lead to employment. You sense that you're entering unexplored territory here. You have a vague idea of what the pay range is within the company for jobs of this kind, but most of your evidence is anecdotal or hearsay. The negotiation is imminent and you probably ought to do a bit of research, but how?

Job Search Principle to Follow

Research pays off.

Before you are too deeply into the interviewing process, you will want to do some research to find out what the going salary ranges are within your field and industry. Talk to other people in the field, interview employment counselors, check help-wanted ads in local and out-of-town papers.

Strategic Actions

☞ Contact a professional association that represents people with your field of employment and find out what information or references it can give from recent salary surveys.

☞ Collect employment advertising from local markets and others comparable to the one you're going to be entering. From the range of the salaries advertised, select a target for yourself in the top 20%.

☞ Ask the people you contacted during your information interviewing for advice about the salary ranges in your field.

☞ If you are a recent graduate, consult a knowledgeable counselor at a college or alumni placement office concerning the salary range issue.

9.4 Negotiate Salary

Situation

The employer has informed you that the company works within fixed salary ranges. You feel a little relieved. The employer will calculate the offer, and you will . . .

Job Search Principle to Follow

Negotiate!

When it comes to salary negotiation, especially in the lower and middle levels, even the best job masters make the assumption that the employer knows the limitations of his budget and has a limitless stock of candidates. In our experience only a small percentage of candidates engage in serious salary negotiations. We recommend that you be among them.

☞ Use the following three rules to help you gain leverage in your negotiations:

Rule 1: *Don't make the first bid.*

Do what you can to avoid answering the question, "What is the minimum salary you would accept?" This is a deadly question that no person should have to answer. You can short-circuit this question by asking the employer first, "What is the salary range for this job?" If you are asked the deadly question first, you might respond: "Frankly, I'm not looking for the minimum. I am interested in a job in which I can make a major contribution and be compensated accordingly. By the way, what kind of salary range do you have in mind?"

When responding to advertisements that ask you to state salary requirements or past salary, you will have to respond to this; however, you may not want to answer the question directly. In your cover letter, you might say that the salary is negotiable and you are unable to name a figure until you find out more about the job's responsibilities. If you feel you need to give more information, you might answer generally, for example: "Middle forties." This should give the employer enough of a range to know if you're totally out of the question. Another possibility is to say, "I am willing to work for the current market salary for this job." Remember that you're operating as an equal partner, not as someone needing to be saved from financial disaster. If you *do* need to be saved from financial disaster, it's all the more important to keep a stiff upper lip and negotiate effectively.

Rule 2: *Go for the top of the range.*

If the employer says "the salary range is £35,000–45,000"—and that's within your target—your response should be, "Forty-five thousand is in the ballpark." By verbalizing the top of the range, you eliminate the possibility that you'll inadvertantly get stuck at the lower end of the range. If a salary range is well under your budget you might say: "We'll need to discuss that further, but first let me tell you more about what I'm able to contribute to your firm."

Rule 3: *Never accept the offer when it's given.*

Whenever an offer is given, let the employer know that you're going to take it into consideration and that you need to take four or five days to look at it carefully to make sure you're making the right decision. During those four or five days you should seriously consider why you want to accept the job and see if you have any second thoughts. If you have none, it's time for you to negotiate even further.

$\boxed{9.5}$ DON'T CAVE IN

SITUATION:

You: "I appreciate your offer, but my salary target is 20% higher than the offer. Can you come closer to my target?"
Employer: "Once we make an offer it's almost impossible for us to change it."
You: . . .

JOB SEARCH PRINCIPLE TO FOLLOW

Don't cave in.

In most organizations salary *is* negotiable. This is true even though the employer insists his firm is limited in what it can pay and that salary ranges are rigid, etc. As we said before, money follows value, so if you've demonstrated enough tangible value (for example, in bringing in a contract from a previous situation, in fund raising, in savings costs, etc.), you should find the employer willing to raise the salary or bring you up to another level.

STRATEGIC ACTION

☞ The art of negotiation is a valued skill—one that many employers find quite worthwhile in their candidates. What better way to demonstrate your ability to negotiate than in the course of making a good bargain in your own compensation discussions? Much has been written about the negotiation process. Here are some basic tenets of good negotiating that will help you manage a constructive dialogue about your salary:

- Negotiating is not a win-lose proposition. You want the employer to realize that the bargain goes both ways: you to get well paid, the employer to acquire your great value for the company.

- Don't allow the discussions to get confrontational. By keeping the conversation open, you preserve the relationship as well as the outcome. This makes it easier to negotiate in the future.

- Never say no. When the employer names a figure short of your target, don't blurt out, "No! I can't work for that!" Simply state that you need to consider the offer and get back to him. When you get back to him, tell him what you want to counterpropose.

- Have more than one variable to play with. If the negotiation is only about the raw figure for salary, the negotiation can stalemate quickly, especially when there appears to be little room to move. Bring other elements into the discussion: work schedule, learning opportunities, tuition refund, time for next performance review, etc. Let the employer know early in the negotiating process that you need to be clear about a number of parts of the new relationship so that the introduction of these factors does not come as a surprise.
- Speak of value as a trade-off for money. Keep the conversation about money always focused on the value you can provide the company. Insist that the employer understand the value in the deal.
- Don't play off your needs. Play by your merits.

9.6 WORK STYLE IS NEGOTIABLE

SITUATION

You had a pretty strong start in your career: The work went well, and the employer held out strong promise. Then came the baby, and now the six-month leave is coming to an end. You want your career and professional stature to grow. On the other hand, this little infant pulls at your heartstrings. The big question: Do I return to the 9-to-5 routine or not?

JOB SEARCH PRINCIPLE TO FOLLOW

Work style is negotiable.

The move is on to depressurize jobs, to support family relationships in the work context, and to negotiate nontraditional employment arrangements. In your salary and employment negotiations consider the kinds of hours you want to work, how much time you want to spend at home, the needs of your spouse and children, possibilities for retraining and continuing education, future goals within the company, etc. In other words, rather than simply focus on the amount of a particular salary, look at the larger picture and be prepared to talk about other possibilities for getting the job done.

STRATEGIC ACTIONS

☞ Make a diagram or chart of your current or most recent job, or the job that you've targeted, to analyze how you spend your time: with customers, on the phone, making decisions, processing work, etc. Determine which activities produce the most value for the employer and which provide the least payoff. Which of these high-value tasks require your being in or near the office, and which could be done from home or in an alternative work structure? Look at two or three different ways to redesign the job in terms of time worked in the office and at home, and creative ways to use the work time (ten hours a day, four days a week). Try to come up with a work-style plan that best suits the requirements of both you and the employer. Consider how you'd convince an employer that it is to his advantage to let you work in this way.

☞ Consider consulting and freelance work. Working freelance has advantages for the individual in terms of flexibility, home responsibilities, going to school, building diversified talents, etc. The big disadvantage for many is that there is little guarantee of security, benefits, and a predictable income level. For the employer there are also many advantages: a short-term commitment when the future cannot be predicted, a lower long-term financial investment.

☞ Enhance your own understanding of the consulting field by locating someone who is operating as a consultant: Meet with her and pick her brain. Find out about her approach to marketing, fee rates, referrals, work style, etc. See if you can find some rationale whereby working as a consultant would create a greater benefit to the employer than working in a more traditional way.

9.7 BREAK OUT OF A SALARY

SITUATION

Early in your career you kept your mouth shut when you should have negotiated for a higher salary, or you took a lower-paying job in a nonprofit organization, or you started a job at a certain level of skill and have since increased it significantly. In any case, today you find that your salary is significantly below the norm for people with equivalent skills and experiences, and each successive salary increase is calculated on that basis. You need to catch up—but how?

JOB SEARCH PRINCIPLE TO FOLLOW

Break out of salary traps.

Whether they are looking for a new job or not, many people at mid-career find themselves earning substantially less than other people of the same age and with equivalent education. Whatever the reason you got there, you need to address the problem directly and do what you can to bring your salary up to market level.

STRATEGIC ACTIONS

☞ Research to compare the requirements of your current position with others in the field. Build a case for the salary you want. Clearly define the benefits of your employment to the employer.

☞ After what you consider to have been a successful interview, and before the salary discussions have started, tell the employer, "I'd like you to know that I consider the salary I've been earning in the past two jobs to be substantially under what I'm worth and what the market is paying. This is because I spent too much time in a nonprofit organization, doing what I consider to be quite excellent work, but working at lower pay than I can afford to right now. In our discussions here, I intend to keep my salary in the current market range and not based on my past." By saying this early in the negotiation, you've forewarned the employer and you avoid a situation in which you get an offer based on your previous low salary. It's more difficult to negotiate out of the range once it has been established.

☞ Be OUTRAGEOUS! Break away from any old characterization or assumptions you've had about your earning power. Don't be embarrassed to ask for what you're worth, and beyond. Don't be embarrassed about learning how to generate more worth so that you can then demand a higher salary. People often get stuck in lower salaries and then downgrade their capabilities to the level of the salary. We recommend that you envision yourself doing effective and high-performance work, and that you set your salary target to that vision. Your worth should be based on your operating at 100% of your capability. Constantly improve and develop your capabilities, and your salary and earning power will follow.

References

Outstanding Negotiator Godefroy and Robert (Piatkus)

Getting to Yes Robert Fisher and William Ury (Century)

Getting Past No William Ury (Century)

How to Negotiate Your Salary Alan Jones (Century)

Appendix

Directories

There are literally thousands of directories; here are some of the most common ones:

ABC Europe
British Rate & Data (Brad)—a directory of press publications
Directory of British Associations
Directory of Directors—details on 58,000 UK board members
Dun & Bradstreet Guide to Key British Enterprises—20,000 companies
Dun & Bradstreet International Market Guide—Continental Europe
Dun & Bradstreet Principal International Businesses
Financial Times International Business Yearbook—700 international companies
Handbook of Market Leaders
Inter-Company Comparisons—performance data on top companies in 70
    markets
Jordan Dataquest—a directory of 12,000 companies
Kelly's Business Directory
Kompass—directories for all key countries, classified by industry, location,
    products and services, with details of senior managers
Sources of Economic Information
Times 1000 Companies
Who Owns Whom—ownership data on subsidiary companies
Whitaker's Almanack—comprehensive listing of business, trade and research
    associations, financial institutions and media.

Superdirectories

For information on other directories, look at the following superdirectories:

Current British Directories—covers almost all categories of directory
List of Lists
Top 3000 Directories & Annuals
Trade Associations & Professional Bodies in the UK

Recruitment Directories

The Executive Grapevine
The CEPEC Recruitment Guide

Piatkus Business Books

Piatkus Business Books have been created for people who need expert knowledge readily available in a clear and easy-to-follow format. All the books are written by specialists in their field. They will help you improve your skills quickly and effortlessly in the workplace and on a personal level. Titles include:

Presentation and Communication

Better Business Writing Maryann V Piotrowski
Complete Book of Business Etiquette, The Lynne Brennan and David Block
Confident Conversation Dr Lillian Glass
Confident Speaking: how to communicate effectively using the Power Talk System Christian H Godefroy and Stephanie Barrat
He Says, She Says: closing the communication gap between the sexes Dr Lillian Glass
Networking and Mentoring: a woman's guide Dr Lily M Segerman-Peck
Outstanding Negotiator, The Christian H Godefroy and Luis Robert
Personal Power Philippa Davies
Powerspeak: the complete guide to public speaking and presentation Dorothy Leeds
Presenting Yourself: a personal image guide for men Mary Spillane
Presenting Yourself: a personal image guide for women Mary Spillane
Say What You Mean and Get What You Want George R. Walther
Your Total Image Philippa Davies

Careers

How to Find the Perfect Job Tom Jackson
Marketing Yourself: how to sell yourself and get the jobs you've always wanted Dorothy Leeds
Perfect CV, The Tom Jackson
Perfect Job Search Strategies Tom Jackson
Secrets of Successful Interviews Dorothy Leeds
Ten Steps To The Top Marie Jennings
Which Way Now?—how to plan and develop a successful career Bridget Wright

General Management and Business Skills

Best Person for the Job, The Malcolm Bird

Beware the Naked Man Who Offers You His Shirt Harvey Mackay

Be Your Own PR Expert: the complete guide to publicity and public relations Bill Penn

Brain Power: the 12-week mental training programme Marilyn vos Savant and Leonore Fleischer

Complete Conference Organiser's Handbook, The Robin O'Connor

Complete Time Management System, The Christian H Godefroy and John Clark

Confident Decision Making J Edward Russo and Paul J H Schoemaker

Creating Abundance Andrew Ferguson

Creative Thinking Michael LeBoeuf

Dealing with Difficult People Robert Cava

Energy Factor, The: how to motivate your workforce Art McNeil

Firing On All Cylinders: the quality management system for high-powered corporate performance Jim Clemmer with Barry Sheehy

Great Boom Ahead, The Harry Dent

How to Choose Stockmarket Winners Raymond Caley

How to Implement Corporate Change John Spencer and Adrian Pruss

How to Run a Part-Time Business Barrie Hawkins

Influential Manager, The: how to develop a powerful management style Lee Bryce

Leadership Skills for Every Manager Jim Clemmer and Art McNeil

Lure the Tiger Out of the Mountains: timeless tactics from the East for today's successful manager Gao Yuan

Managing Your Team John Spencer and Adrian Pruss

Memory Booster: easy techniques for rapid learning and a better memory Robert W Finkel

Organise Yourself Ronni Eisenberg with Kate Kelly

Perfectly Legal Tax Loopholes Stephen Courtney

Play to Your Strengths Donald O Clifton and Paula Nelson

Problem Employees: how to improve their behaviour and their performance Peter Wylie and Mardy Grothe

Problem Solving Techniques That Really Work Malcolm Bird

Profit Through the Post: How to set up and run a successful mail order business Alison Cork

Psychological Testing for Managers Dr Stephanie Jones

Quantum Learning: unleash the genius within you Bobbi DePorter with Mike Hernacki

Right Brain Manager, The: how to use the power of your mind to achieve personal and professional success Dr Harry Alder

Seven Cultures of Capitalism, The: value systems for creating wealth in Britain, the United States, Germany, France, Japan, Sweden and the Netherlands Charles Hampden-Turner and Alfons Trompenaars

Sharkproof: get the job you want, keep the job you love in today's tough job market Harvey Mackay

Smart Questions for Successful Managers Dorothy Leeds
Strategy of Meetings, The George David Kieffer
10-Day MBA, The Steven Silbiger
Three Minute Meditator, The David Harp with Nina Feldman

Sales and Customer Services

Art of the Hard Sell, The Robert L Shook
Creating Customers David H Bangs
Guerrilla Marketing Excellence Jay Conrad Levinson
How to Close Every Sale Joe Girard
How to Collect the Money You Are Owed Malcolm Bird
How to Succeed in Network Marketing Leonard Hawkins
How to Win Customers and Keep Them for Life Michael LeBoeuf
Making Profits: a six-month plan for the small business Malcolm Bird
Sales Power: the Silva mind method for sales professionals Jose Silva and Ed
    Bernd Jr
Selling Edge, The Patrick Forsyth
Telephone Selling Techniques That Really Work Bill Good
Winning Edge, The Charles Templeton
Winning New Business: a practical guide to successful sales presentations
    Dr David Lewis

For a free brochure with further information on our complete range of business titles, please write to:

Piatkus Books
Freepost 7 (WD 4505)
London W1E 4EZ

PIATKUS